# King of the Road

## Adventures Along New Mexico's
## Friendly Byways

### Lesley S. King

NEW MEXICO
MAGAZINE

# opyright 2007

New Mexico Magazine
www.nmmagazine.com

Author & Photographer: Lesley S. King (www.lesleysking.com)
Maps, Book Design & Production: Bette Brodsky
Editor: Arnold Vigil
Copy Editor: Penny Landay
Publisher: Ethel Hess

Library of Congress PCN Number: 2007929584
ISBN: 978-0-937206-94-2
Printed in China

Cover: Gene Beck's 1957 Corvette in front of the San Marcos Café on the Turquoise Trail.
Cover photo: Steve Larese

Many thanks to Alma, Barbara Doolittle, Elbert King, Steve Larese, Emily Drabanski, Jon
Bowman, Terry Tiedeman, Arnold Vigil, Bette Brodsky, and all the wonderful people I
encountered on these and other journeys.

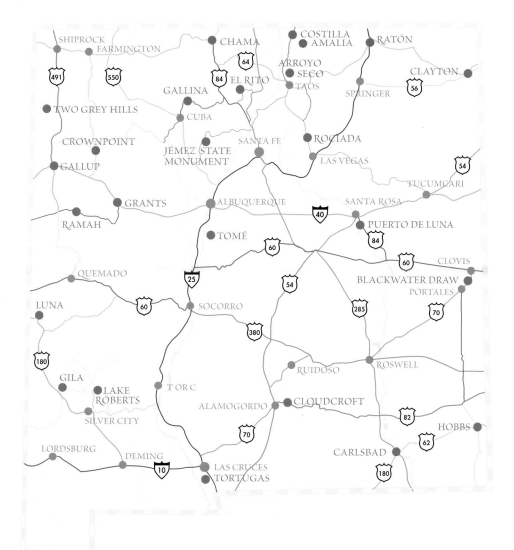

# able of Contents

## INTRODUCTION

TRAVELERS TODAY SEEK A DEEPER EXPERIENCE THAN WHAT'S OFFERED BY MOST TRAVEL GUIDES AND TOUR SERVICES. THEY WANT TO FEEL LIKE THEY'RE PENETRATING A CULTURE OR A PLACE, THEREBY FINDING ADVENTURE AND GAINING NEW UNDERSTANDING OF THE WORLD.

That's what this book, *King of the Road*, accomplishes. We take readers to Two Grey Hills to meet master weaver Clara Sherman, to the Gallup Flea Market to taste a mutton sandwich and to Lake Roberts to hear the flutter of a hummingbird's heart. We cruise Ratón's hidden historic district to find relics of railroad history and delve into villages on the edge of the San Pedro Wilderness in search of the ancient Gallina Warriors.

These travel essays arose from my "King of the Road" column, which has appeared in *New Mexico Magazine* for nearly five years. As well as presenting adventures that travelers can take, these essays give practical information: a historic century-old plaza near the Colorado border in Costilla or a café in El Rito that serves some of the world's best chicken enchiladas. You'll also find suggestions on things to enhance your journey, such as reading *Viva Guadalupe!* to help understand the Fiesta of Our Lady of Guadalupe in Tortugas. Some of the *King of the Road* essays focus on an event, such as the "World's Biggest Small Town Rodeo" in Luna, or "Christmas on the Pecos" in Carlsbad. Each chapter has a map pinpointing the town's location.

The tone of the book is fun, at times pensive, and even a little nostalgic. I was born in New Mexico, raised on a ranch in the northeastern part of the state and have lived most of my half-century of years here, experiences which help me interweave stories and anecdotes into the adventures. But what's most unique about his book is its process. I go to these towns and knock on residents' doors. They invite me into their kitchens that smell of posole and anise and tell me their stories and the tales of their towns.

With *New Mexico Magazine* as my emissary — a magazine that everyone loves — I'm always welcome. I also draw strongly from my work writing *Frommer's Travel Guides*, a job which takes me all over the Southwest, where I like to say — jokingly — that I "eat and sleep around," because I check out so many restaurants and accommodations. After over a decade of such "work," as well as experience writing for magazines, which has taken me to Costa Rica, Italy, France, Eastern Europe and the Middle East, I've developed a strong criteria for where to eat and stay, and a good idea of what makes for a fun and interesting time on the road.

So, join me as we take 24 adventures, along Route 66, *El Camino Real* and beyond, exploring the back ways of this glorious Land of Enchantment.

A freelance writer, editor and photographer, Lesley S. King is a contributor to *The New York Times, Audubon Magazine,* United Airlines *Hemispheres* magazine, *La Vie Claire* and other publications. A former editor of *The Santa Fean,* she has a monthly travel column in *New Mexico Magazine,* and she is the author of a number of travel guide books, including *Frommer's New Mexico, Frommer's American Southwest* and *New Mexico for Dummies.* Her *Farm Fresh Journey: The Santa Fe Farmers' Market Cookbook* will be released in summer 2008.

orth Central

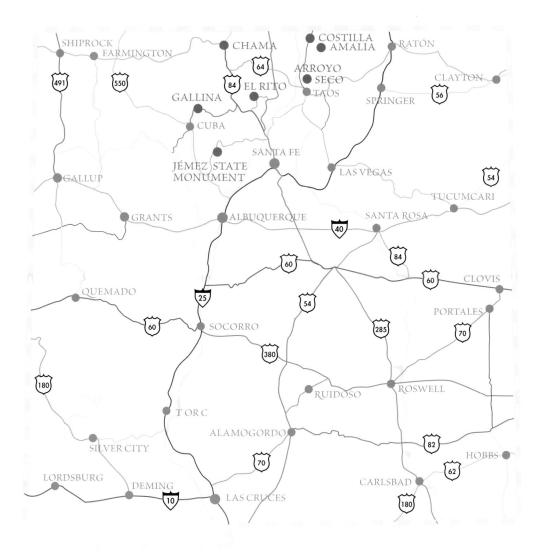

## DAWN COMES TO ARROYO SECO

FOR ALMOST A HALF-CENTURY I'VE TRAVELED THROUGH ARROYO SECO EN ROUTE TO AND FROM TAOS SKI VALLEY. MOST OF THOSE YEARS IT WAS LITTLE BUT A SHARP TURN IN THE ROAD. BUT IT HAS RECENTLY AWAKENED, AS THOUGH FROM A LONG SLEEP, TO SUDDENLY FIND ITSELF A HAPPENING PLACE.

*Artist Scott Carlson makes a pot on the porch of his gallery in the center of town.*

My mother and I see the first signs of this awakening at Abe's *Cantina y Cocina,* where Olympia and Lina Garcia are setting up for the day. They're industrious women, both with short hair and lovely olive skin. Fourth generation Arroyo Secoans, they grew up behind the *Cantina,* a thriving spot since 1945.

Throughout the years, the place has become renowned, not only as a local bar, but also as a restaurant. In fact, visitors arrive with coolers to take Lina's tamales home to places all over the United States. And word-of-mouth brings others in for breakfast burritos.

"One woman came from Louisiana and said a friend had told her she had to eat one here," says Olympia as she breaks open a head of lettuce.

Back out on the street, we're surprised to find not a lazy village as one might suspect, but a place bustling with trucks and drivers unloading liquor and packages of cupcakes for the store. Across the street, they deliver furniture and knickknacks, the air scented with exhaust smoke.

Meanwhile, down the street, we come upon Scott Carlson, an easygoing artist who sits on a porch surrounded by an adobe wall, his hands sticky with clay. He leans over a potting wheel to pull up the sides of a vase he's making and explains that about four years ago the town really came alive, with real estate prices reflecting the change.

"Taos Pueblo borders it on one side and Spanish land grants line it on the other," Scott says. "So it can't really grow outward."

Instead it's becoming more textured. Back out on the main street, the trucks have gone and the light has grown dramatic. To the west stand the Taos Mountains, a place where waterfalls pour in the spring and many feet of snow stand through the winter. Now, billowing clouds hang above the forested peaks, lending their brightness to the colors of the village, little galleries and shops displaying sculptures and clothes in azure, persimmon and chartreuse.

Our attention goes to skeins of yarn hanging on a hitching post at Taos Sunflower. As a knitter, my mother quickly christens this shop one of the Seven Wonders of the World.

Even non-knitters like me are transported to some kind of bliss by the colors here. Hip, textured and brilliant yarns sit in bins and on shelves and hang from cords tied to the windows.

Shop owner Martie Moreno, a classic earth mother, sells yarn and needles, and gives advice to customers finding their way here from all over. She also convenes groups of knitters. The members range in age from 20-somethings to grandmothers, who click-clack away. "We often make charity blankets for people struggling with illness," Martie says.

Next we head into Doug West Gallery to see West's monumental landscapes, as well as some delicate shell-like pottery by local Carole Ross. Nearby, at Arroyo Seco Mercantile, we explore fully. The store has the feel of an early 1900s dry-goods shop, but with a contemporary eclectic selection. Cowboy hats and antique *trasteros* mingle with New Age CDs and natural, handmade "Hogwash" soap. My mother buys a birdhouse shaped like a cathedral to add to her collection.

Tucked away behind the mercantile is a stunning church. Built in 1834, the *Santísima Trinidad* was restored in 1990. It has thick, hand-rubbed adobe walls, which stand gracefully below a pitched tin roof. Inside, wood floors creak under our feet and large, high windows illuminate the altar screen, a colorful, imaginative work painted by José de Gracia Gonzales.

We finish our Arroyo Seco visit on the patio of Gypsy 360° Café, with big thunderheads rumbling above us. The restaurant reflects the boldness of this town's spirit, serving some of the best contemporary world cuisine in the region at prices that let you order heartily.

As I bite into a grilled salmon sandwich and my mother savors her bacon blue cheeseburger, we smile at each other, glad to be a part of the awakening of the village of "dry creek."

*Hidden on a backstreet, the* Santísima Trinidad *was restored in 1990.*

*Inside and out, the* Santísima Trinidad *is a model northern New Mexico church.*

# HOBNOBBING WITH RAILROADIES IN THE NEW CHAMA

SOMETHING INTERESTING HAPPENS IN THE MIDST OF CHANGE. IT'S EVIDENT IN A PREGNANT WOMAN'S FACE, OR IN THE AIR OF A FRIEND IN LOVE. THEY GLOW WITH THE LIGHT OF POSSIBILITY. THE SAME CAN BE SEEN IN A TOWN.

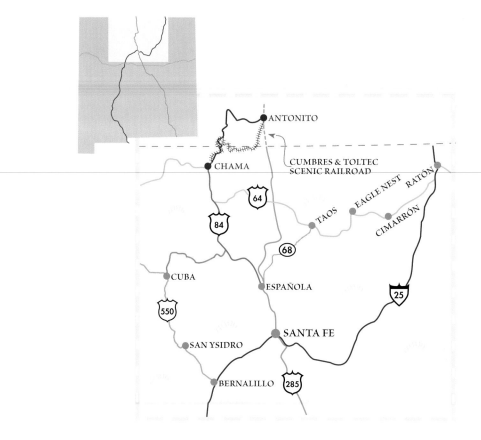

I notice it immediately when I drive into the northern New Mexico village of Chama. The place seems . . . happy. And, it has — drum-roll please — sidewalks, which it has never had before. Those details are what first come into view in this railroad town that for years has worn a rough pallor. Curbside parking slots make it easy to pull up to little shops — some new, some revamped — and look around.

*The Cumbres & Toltec Scenic Railroad yards provide a living museum experience.*

I stumble on a shop that sells espresso and cappuccino, locals sipping theirs while strolling past new street lamps and a 17-foot-tall clock tower. It's been erected in the high point of all this change, a city park stretching through the center of town, with grass, trees and views down into the railyard.

For a place that's been marked by hardship, this glow of change is notable. With only a 108-day growing season, followed by snowy winters, Chama hasn't had much to rely on for industry. It's held tight to the Cumbres & Toltec Scenic Railroad as its main source, and a not-so-stable one at that. "That's the only reason Chama exists. It came into being because of the train," says Chris Novak, who works for the railroad.

We head down into the railyard, a living museum of sorts, where the guts of the railroad stand bare. It's true, in a sense, the history of Chama is the history of the railroad. Prior to the coming of the Denver and Rio Grande Western Railway in 1880, it was but a crossroads settlement. Now, it's a town of around 1,199 inhabitants.

"Push that lever with your foot," says Orlando Ulibarri, as I stand in the cockpit of a train engine. I do as he says and, bam, a door opens to a cauldron so fiery I jump back. This is no pretend railroading experience, I note as I climb off the engine and continue my tour through the yards with Chris.

"It's very authentic," Chris says. "We're not doing a showpiece. You'd be hard pressed to find a living museum with this many pieces anywhere."

*The Cumbres & Toltec Scenic Railroad offers a scenic ride over the 10,022-foot Cumbres Pass and into Antonito, Colo.*

He's right. The railroad yard is alive today, with people working and visitors wandering around taking pictures of the 1899 depot and the 1924 coal tipple, the only one of its kind that's still functional.

Though the railroad, which takes visitors on an incredibly scenic jaunt from Chama to Antonito, Colo., is world-renowned, it's no cash cow. The biggest hardship comes in maintaining it. In the machine shop, Chris shows me a stripped-down engine. Because of government regulations and the wear and tear of time, all the Cumbres & Toltec engines are in line to be rebuilt, with two completed thus far. At a cost of $1.3 million each, that's no small task.

"It's a feat of galactic proportions that we have two full-fledged engines running now," says Chris.

Locals thank Gov. Bill Richardson for helping bring money to the train.

"Last year, without his help, the train would not have run," says historian Margaret Palmer, a Chama resident for 31 years, who we meet up with along the way. "The end of the railroad would mean the end of Chama."

For the changes in the town, she credits a new government. "We finally have a really decent city council interested in making Chama nice for locals and tourists."

For lending hope to the whole place, everyone seems to credit the Friends of the Cumbres & Toltec Scenic Railroad. Some 2,000 railroadies from all over the world rotate visits to Chama to do volunteer work. They rebuild train cars, maintain buildings, and donate time and money to other local projects.

"We work on the historic aspect," says Bob Tully, a volunteer from Denver. "Our interest is in preservation, interpretation and education, but we do anything to keep it going."

"It's so much fun!" adds volunteer Nan Clark from Floresville, Texas. Such is the attitude of many, whether Friends of the Railroad or simply locals.

Margaret Palmer and her husband Clif consider themselves true railroadies. "It's the romance of the west," says Margaret. "We travel all over the world to ride railroads, but there's nothing that equals Chama."

A pastime of railroadies is "chasing the train," an activity some like almost as much as riding it. They find out where it crosses the road and race to take pictures there. "Well, you know, we need a few more railroad shots," Margaret says, satirically. "After taking thousands."

Before retiring, Clif worked 10 years for the railroad. He, like many, listens to the train talk. "It's like Morse code," he says of the whistle. What sounds like nonsense horn blowing is actually a whole train language. For instance, two long toots means the train is moving forward, while three means it's moving backwards, among many other variations.

"Especially when it's in the yard, people need to know what the train is doing," Cliff adds. For me, train whistles will never sound the same again.

And I won't look at Chama the same either. As well as changing its look, the town is expanding its attractions. A chuckwagon cowboy dinner show now livens up the evenings, and some new terrain expands the already vast cross-country ski options. For railroadies, a parlor car on the Cumbres & Toltec makes for a more luxurious ride north to Antonito.

Suddenly, the train engine toots — two long whistles — and I know it's moving forward.

## COSTILLA & AMALIA:
### Journey into Shadow and Light

THE BEAUTY OF TRAVELING IS IN STOPPING. NOT JUST PAUSING, BUT REALLY SETTING YOUR FEET DOWN IN A PLACE, LOOKING AROUND AND LISTENING TO THE STORIES IT HAS TO TELL. THAT'S WHAT MY MOTHER AND I DO ON A STORMY WINTER DAY THAT BLOWS US AGAINST THE COLORADO BORDER IN THE VILLAGES OF COSTILLA AND AMALIA.

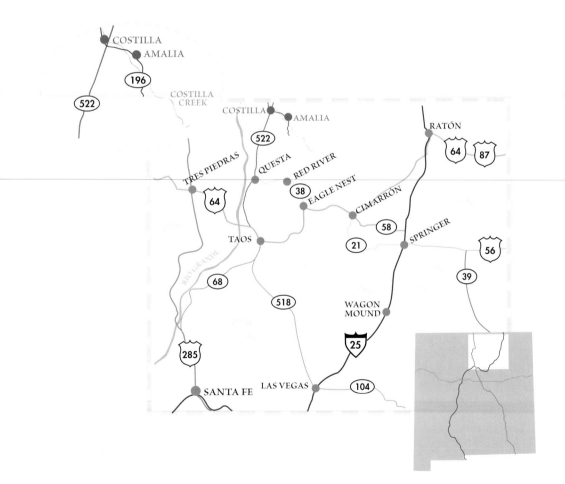

*Bernie Torres, an enterprising fourth-generation resident of the area, ships "high country hay" to places as far away as Florida and California.*

N̲ew Mexico highway 196 passes through Costilla, cutting between some old adobe buildings that at first seem of little note. Or so I think, until Bernie Torres, a fourth-generation resident of the area, stops me and points out the way they form a lovely quadrangle called *Plaza de Arriba*. They're partly dilapidated, yes, but today also partly restored. Upon recognizing this plaza built in 1849, I find the whole area takes on dimension, the stories that follow adding even more shadow and light.

The area is most known for Ski Rio, an enterprise that from the early 1980s well into the 1990s struggled to survive and finally closed. But those years are just a snowflake on a vast northern New Mexico landscape, where the history is really about logging, sheepherding and cattle grazing.

"Dad came from Taos herding sheep through the mountains," says Bernie, while we stand outside watching storm clouds tangle up with the peaks of the Sangre de Cristos. "He went with a friend to a dance in Amalia. They met two sisters and married them."

That family history, which started with such romance, became the reality of life in the north. In subsequent years, Bernie's father left during the winters to work coal mines in Colorado, while his mother took care of eight kids. This was in the 1950s, but while most families in the United States were enjoying Amana ranges and refrigerators, those in Amalia lived without electricity and telephones.

"All our meals we canned from the summer garden, or dried," says Bernie. "We had a cellar full of potatoes, canned peaches and beef jerky."

He sings a song his mother wrote to the tune of *"Las Mañanitas:"*

> *En mi casita en Amalia*
> *Donde yo me crié,*
> *Tengo muchas memorias*
> *Que nunca olivdaré.*

*Dating from 1849, the Plaza de Arriba in Costilla, presents a picture of the hardship of 19th century life. Within its walls residents once secured their farm animals against attacks by Plains tribes.*

*In my little house in Amalia*
*Where I was born,*
*I have many memories*
*I will never forget.*

The song goes on to tell how his mother was raised, how she learned to pray and to respect people. "I get choked up when my family sings it," Bernie says. "Because of the love of our parents for all they had to endure."

Before us, the plaza itself tells a story of endurance. At one corner, bare adobes crumble under the elements. The south segment is at times livelier, with businesses that tend to come and go. The eastern section has been restored by Bernie, the rooms quaint, with coved vigas and kiva fireplaces.

Saying goodbye to him, we head farther up the valley in search of the village in the song, Amalia. We follow the Río Costilla as it curves and gurgles along meadows and through cottonwood stands. Then the canyon broadens and there sits the village, a cluster of adobe houses surrounding the white Santo Niño Church, a modest place with an image of *Santo Niño de Atoche* out front.

We make our way to the home of Alfonso and Carolyn Gonzales, where Carolyn and her little grandson Cameron greet us.

*The Santo Niño Church adorns the center of the agrarian village of Amalia.*

Carolyn met Alfonso 47 years ago in her hometown, Alamosa, Colo., then moved to his home, Amalia. When she got here, they set about making adobe bricks by hand to build their home. "With horses we plowed the dirt and we put in straw and water," she says. They built the first few rooms and added on over the years as more children came. The home is surrounded by alfalfa fields and crowned by a small lake. Nearby, trailers and homes stand where Carolyn and Alfonso's children and grandchildren live.

Like many in the area, they subsist on ranching, farming and other jobs, such as teaching school and hauling wood. The Gonzaleses are part of the Río Costilla Cooperative Livestock Association, which has 180 members who run cattle and hunt on nearly 80,000 acres. The association also opens their land to visitors, who fish and hike on rich terrain that includes the noted Latir Lakes.

Today, Carolyn is busy drying pumpkin seeds and celery leaves, her entry hall piled with gourds, winter squash and late-season tomatoes. While snow flurries outside and wind blows the storm deeper into the canyon, she takes us to their little lake, where people pay to fish for trout in summer.

She points across to a parcel of land bordering the highway. "That's where Alfonso's sister lives," she says, and in the gesture I can see illustrated the story of this land. Settled centuries ago, it's been passed down and parceled out to kids and their kids, who work it and do whatever other jobs they can find, the traditions changing and yet continuing.

ON A CLOUDLESS AUTUMN DAY, I SET OUT
ALONG N.M. 96 WITH ABSOLUTELY NO INTEN-
TION EXCEPT TO SEE WHAT EXISTS IN PLACES
WITH SUCH FERAL NAMES AS COYOTE AND
GALLINA.

*In Coyote, Santana V. Salazar still weaves the way her grandfather taught her.*

I know they're outposts on the edge of the remote San Pedro Parks Wilderness. I've heard foreboding tales — that outsiders are scorned and that mysterious ruins of Gallina Warriors hide among the red and yellow cliffs.

The trip starts with washes of color — the blue of Abiquiú Lake, the yellow, red and gray of towering cliffs, and the green anvil-shaped *Cerro Pedernal*, which always seems to be present in this area, no matter how many corners one turns.

Farther along, like eggs in a golden nest, the village of Coyote lies in a valley of cottonwoods at the convergence of Coyote Creek and the Río Puerco. I make my way down a dirt road to a contemporary church surrounded by houses with untended apple orchards and monstrous piles of wood.

The wood is symbolic of the life most lead here on the edge of the 42,132-acre San Pedro, with peaks climbing to 10,624 feet. Winters are cold here, and people heat their homes with wood they themselves cut from local forests.

Back on N.M. 96, I stop at Santana V. Salazar's weaving shop. Fortunately, Santana and her son Ron are in. Even without her poetic name, Santana is interesting, with her aged face still revealing high cheekbones, her no-nonsense attitude and hands lily soft from oil in the wool.

*"Mi abuelo, Juan Manuel Velásquez, era tejedor,"* she explains. Her grandfather was a weaver, and she still weaves many of his designs, as well as her own, using mostly natural dyes made from local ingredients such as chamisa and wild spinach. The rugs are lovely, striped with rich reds, browns and greens. She's sold them to people from all over the world and seems almost perplexed with the notion that some now hang on walls in places such as Japan and Argentina.

The highway climbs out of Coyote into ponderosa forest, which opens to high meadows. At one such meadow I stop to see a sight only available in autumn. Far on a hillside, a patch of aspens shines yellow, creating an image of what looks like a panther or leopard

Left: *As with most northern New Mexico cemeteries, the locals adorn the sites with plastic and silk flowers.*

Opposite: *Cerro Pedernal seems to stand always present, no matter how many corners one turns.*

leaping at full run. It was likely the inspiration for Gallina's Coronado High School mascot, the leopard — a better choice than the town's namesake, a hen or chicken.

My first encounter upon entering the village of Gallina, which is more modern than Coyote, is a dead elk. It's not an uncommon sight in rural mountain towns where residents hunt for their meat. Chris Lovato, who now dresses it, calls it a "five-by-five," meaning it has five points on each of its antlers. "He would have been a lot bigger if it hadn't been for the drought," Chris says.

"My dad shoots it and I eat it," says a little boy at my next stop, the Gallina Elementary School. I'm visiting a classroom, where I ask what the kids like to eat. Their answers aren't exactly what you'd hear in middle-America: "Deer hamburgers because of the wild taste. Deer fajitas, elk meat chile, fried deer backstraps (marinated in tomato sauce), and *carne seca* made with elk."

At the school I run into Gene McCracken, a math teacher and local guide, who takes me for a ride in his big four-wheel-drive. ("Everybody needs at least one, just to get to their house.") He shows me the Gallina cemetery, set on the bank of a lush valley with

blue mountains in the distance. Locals have adorned the stone and wooden crosses with bright plastic roses and carnations.

Gene tells how things work up here: No backhoe at this mountain site — the graves are dug by friends the night before the service. "Everybody brings a shovel to the burial to cover it up," he says.

A guide in the San Pedro, Gene knows the surrounding mountains and the ancient Native American dwellings scattered throughout them, most accessed by horseback rides or hikes. Though dated at around the time of Chaco Canyon, the ruins in this area are unique because they have 20- to 30-foot-tall towers. In 1933, noted archaeologist Frank Hibbin found 500 such towers spread over an area of 35 to 50 miles, and guarded by intact skeletons belonging to what became known as the "Gallina People." Evidence of fighting led to the nickname, the "Gallina Warriors."

As I head for home through the stunning beauty of dusk, I imagine those warriors, standing guard at their towers. They seem to have done a good job of discouraging interlopers — even today, few people come here.

# JONESING FOR GREEN CHILE IN EL RITO

I CONFESS.

I'LL DRIVE HOURS FOR GOOD CHILE. NOT THAT I EVER HAVE TO IN NEW MEXICO, WHERE IT'S ALMOST AS COMMON AS SUNSHINE. BUT THE IDEA IS THAT I CAN, AND THE JOURNEY IS, OF COURSE, HALF THE FUN.

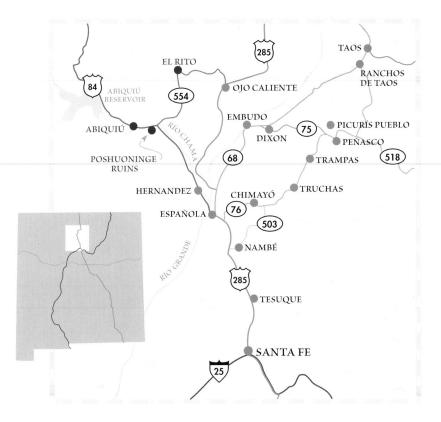

So that's what sends my mother and me to El Rito, the little village near Abiquiú in northern New Mexico, on a cool day, with a storm threatening on the horizon. We're bold, won't be deterred from exploring ancient ruins, slipping into remote galleries and slurping down some good green chile.

An elaborate altar to the Virgin Mary forms the heart of El Rito village.

Advice from a friend takes us en route to a little-known Ancestral Pueblo ruin sitting atop a shelf above the Chama River. *Poshuoninge* (Po-su-in-ge) is a real find for those of us pretend archaeologists with enough imagination to see buildings when looking at unexcavated rock piles.

A fairly steep quarter-mile trail leads up to the first shelf, where stones lie in formation and also randomly scattered, demarking what from A.D. 1400 to 1500 was a town, its inhabitants related to today's local Pueblo tribes.

The trail climbs a quarter-mile farther onto an upper shelf where an artistic rendering of the village aids the imagination in picturing a row of buildings perched on the edge of a cliff below. On the top shelf, there's also a circle of stones, which archaeologists believe was cleared as a work area, with evidence of a hearth and stone tool fragments found there.

From *Poshuouinge* we drive N.M. 554 along the El Rito drainage, with stunning glimpses of hoodoo formations and regal cottonwood stands, into sage country and El Rito village.

The anchor of the place is Northern New Mexico Community College. The campus offers some unique courses of study, including weaving, Spanish Colonial furniture making and building with adobes. We cruise past the suede-colored stucco buildings into the heart of town.

There on a central plaza of sorts is an elaborate altar. Its entryway reads *"Virgen Morena, Ruega Por Nosotros,"* which means Brunette Virgin, Pray For Us. Inside a courtyard

*The first Spanish settlers to the area in the early 1800s built the Church of San Juan Nepomuceño, a graceful example of a northern New Mexico mission.*

stands a statue of the Virgin Mary, her altar draped in plastic roses. It was built in 1957 by Crosio Trujillo, father of the notable green-chile chef we're on a mission to find.

Next door stands what many consider one of the region's finest examples of historic northern New Mexico churches. The Church of San Juan Nepomuceño was built by the first Spanish settlers to the area from 1827 to 1832. With 5-foot thick walls and tiny windows, it served not only as a place of worship, but also as a defensive fort in the frontier town.

Farther down the street we stroll into Martin's Store, a prime example of a small-town market. Greg Martin, the proprietor, tells stories handed down from his grandfather, who moved from New York to the village in the early 1900s to heal from tuberculosis.

He, like many in the region, took up sheep ranching, later opening the store that's still in the family. In Greg's office, which sits above shelves of canned green beans and bags of flour, he shows us photos of the early days in El Rito. It's a smattering of adobe buildings with a thick track through the center, horse carriages stalled in the mud. "To get to Española was a major trip," he says, referring to the town just 30 miles away.

Still an outpost of sorts, El Rito is on the way to nowhere except some lovely, remote sections of the Carson National Forest. But for most who live here, that's exactly the point.

Potter Barbara Campbell moved here 25 years ago hoping to escape the rapid development of California and Colorado. Her plan for life was to be a foreign diplomat, but she took a pottery class and her goals changed.

"I came to El Rito and found a house that had everything I didn't want in a house, then I went to a local bar, met a guy and married him." She's lived in El Rito ever since.

*Dennis Trujillo and his son Dominic run* El Farolito, *which has been written up in* Gourmet, Travel and Leisure *and, most recently,* Rand McNally's Best of the Road.

"I like the remoteness," she adds.

That passion for open space is reflected in her stunning turquoise and ocean blue-glazed pots with imprints of pueblos and plants, which she shows within a cozy room with a coved ceiling in the center of town. She's one of many artists in the area, including traditional Spanish folk artists, a jeweler, calligrapher, basket weaver, tin worker and blacksmith, to name only a few. All share their work during the El Rito Studio Tour, the third weekend in October.

We save the best for last. Hungry and thirsty after all our exploring and chatting up the locals, we step into the noted *El Farolito* at the center of town. In some feat of magic, inside the tiny building is a full-fledged restaurant, with picnic tables lining the walls and rich scents drifting from the kitchen. The remote place has been written about by such authorities as *Gourmet* and *Travel and Leisure*. Most recently, it garnered a recommendation in the *Rand McNally's Best of the Road*.

Dennis Trujillo has been serving up chile at this spot for more than 20 years with the help of his wife, Carmen, and kids, most notably his son Dominic. The Trujillos' ancestors were some of the first to settle the area back in the 1800s.

The family makes some of the best green chile in the state (which, of course, means the world, since nowhere else has chile like we do). It's great in a bowl, or served over enchiladas. We have it both ways, my mom and I lapping it up like a couple of starving waifs.

Meanwhile, Dennis looks on from the kitchen. The flavors sing of passion for cooking, and no wonder. When I ask him if he likes what he does, his answer is simple: "I look forward to it every day."

# PUEBLO REVOLT ECHOES AT JÉMEZ STATE MONUMENT

"OUR BATTLE FOR INDEPENDENCE WAS A SUCCESS. WE ARE A SOVEREIGN NATION AND OUR ANCESTORS WILL BE HERE IN ANOTHER 450 YEARS TO DECLARE THE SAME."

WITH THOSE WORDS THE FIRST LIEUTENANT OF JÉMEZ PUEBLO OPENS THE PUEBLO INDEPENDENCE DAY COMMEMORATION AT JÉMEZ STATE MONUMENT.

*Peter Tafoya, from Jémez, easily finishes the 13-mile footrace that started at his pueblo and ended at the monument.*

**U**nder a cobalt sky, members of many Pueblo tribes, ranging from Taos to Santo Domingo to Jémez, have convened to pay tribute to the day in 1680 when their ancestors rose up against the Spanish colonists and drove them from the land.

It's a day of joy here at Giusewa, the 700-year-old village named for the hot springs that surround it. The festivities include a footrace, food, arts and crafts booths, and music and dancing. I watch thunderheads form around the mountaintops while vendors set up booths to sell Indian tacos, Frito pies and soda pop. It seems that everywhere I turn, I see the fruits of the revolt.

"The Jémez were one of the prime planners of the Pueblo Revolt," explains Rick Reycraft, superintendent of Jémez State Monument, who I meet up with at the edge of the ruins. "At the time this was one of their major villages. A lot of what happened during the revolt, happened here."

I ponder this as I wander through the ruins, adobe walls of homes and kivas that the Jémez people left after the revolt, moving to more defensible places nearby.

Suddenly, the first runner appears. He's followed by others, all having made their way 13 miles from Jémez Pueblo to here. Some wear modern nylon shorts and tank tops, while others run in cotton gym clothes and have bells strapped to their ankles and wrists. Jémez Pueblo is famous for its runners. It's a tribal rite, meant to cleanse the spirit.

One of them, Peter Tafoya, stretches his legs in the middle of what was once the *San José de los Jémez*, a grand mission church constructed in the 17th century using Pueblo labor. It seems poignant to see Peter, so fit and free today, walking among these ruins. He explains that he used to weigh 285 pounds, but then he started running and his life changed completely. With a barely winded voice, he says that he often runs more than 8 miles per day, and that he competes in competitions around the Southwest.

"I run for the tribe," Peter says, "to be strong as a tribe, to keep the family strong."

With the doughy scent of cooking bread filling the air, I make my way over to where Marlene Gachupin of Jémez cooks fry bread in hot oil. She stretches the dough, drops it in

*Near Jémez State Monument clouds form over Red Mesa.*

and then turns it with a stick fashioned from Apache plume. She's her own boss today, working in a place where her ancestors once labored as slaves.

"I usually sell at Red Rocks at the pueblo," Marlene says. "But this is a special day."

I make my way along the arts booths, my eyes flirting with richly veined turquoise necklaces, silver bracelets and hand-smoothed coil pots. At one table I encounter Marlon Magdalena and Audrey Weebothe. Marlon's grandmothers were Jémez potters, but he emerged into the art through painting, which is apparent from the images of nature on the pots he and Audrey make. The Pueblo people's connection to the earth forms the foundation for their spiritual life, which they were able to recapture after the revolt.

"We make owls to watch over us," says Audrey, "and we use frogs as symbols of fertility." The lilt of a flute interrupts us, and soon it's joined by a hollow gourd percussion as the band Cumulonimbus begins a traditional storytelling song. This group of some 10 musicians lays out the tale of a boy who hears wind blow through a willow branch that a bird has carved with holes. The singer ends:

"This is how the first flute was brought to us by the Great Spirit and why you see a little carving on top of each one."

By now the plaza has filled with people buying crafts, licking snow cones and basking in the sun. But all faces turn when the boom of a drum echoes through the narrow San Diego Canyon. Two mysterious creatures with shaggy, horned heads pad onto the dirt. They wear moccasins, white skirts and have fox pelts dangling behind them.

At first moving with a lumbering buffalo pace, they soon become more graceful, brandishing bows and arrows, leaping in the air and acting out the hunt, while the summer sun casts their lively shadows on the earth.

Those shadows and the drumbeats echo the outcome of the Pueblo Revolt. Twelve years later, the Spanish returned to this land, but clearly the Pueblo people had made their point.

*Amongst a crowd and the Jémez ruins, dancers portray the ritual of the hunt in the Buffalo Dance.*

*Marlene Gachupin cooks fry bread at the celebration.*

# Northeast

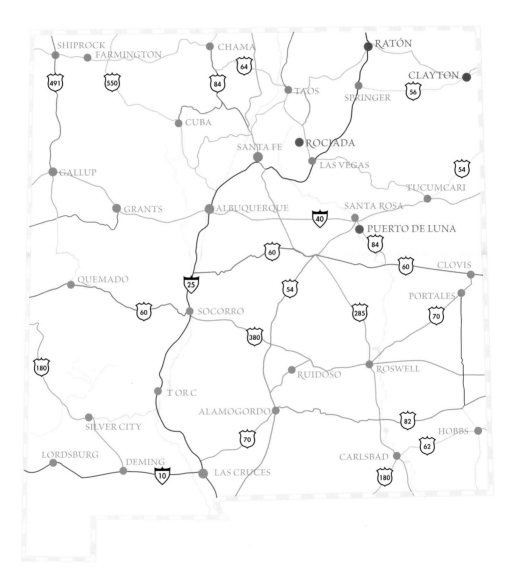

# CLAYTON'S BROAD VIEW OF THE UNIVERSE

CLAYTON IS ON THE ADVENTURE TRAVELER'S RADAR SCREEN NOW, NOT SO MUCH FOR WHAT IT HAS — WHICH IS PLENTY — BUT FOR WHAT IT LACKS: AMBIENT LIGHT. SET IN NORTHEAST-ERN NEW MEXICO, FAR FROM ANY CITY, IT'S A STARGAZER'S DREAM.

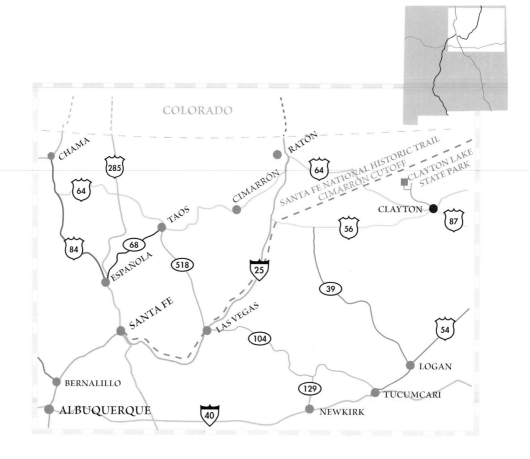

R ight now, though, in the mid-afternoon, everything is bright as I stare through a sunscope. I've managed to visit this town during a relatively rare astronomical phenomenon — when Mercury is passing between the Earth and our sun.

*Chelsea Kear gazes at stars through the telescope as Terrell Jones looks on.*

"You may never see this again in your lifetime," says Terrell Jones, principal of the Clayton Middle School, where we are now. He's also an astrology teacher at the local community college, and has a great passion for stars. "It will happen again, but it might not be visible in this part of the world, or it might be cloudy," he says. "Everything's got to work, including our local weather."

Through the scope, I scan the fiery red sun before me, with solar flares licking out from its surface. And then I see it, at about 1 o'clock on the face, a little black speck, an actual planet — Mercury — visible in daylight. It appears still, but as the afternoon passes, the planet makes its way across the sun.

This scope is a tool of the recently installed $85,000 Star Point Observatory at Clayton Lake State Park, just outside town. The main part of the observatory is a large refractor telescope. "It's the same design as the Hubble Space Telescope," Terrell explains, as he shows middle school students the Mercury phenomenon. I step away and head into the center of Clayton, with plans to meet up with Terrell tonight for a star party.

Cruising the main drag of this one-stoplight town, I find a few interesting galleries and shops, a classic hardware store, and, of course, the historic Eklund Hotel, recently restored and now, with its restaurant and saloon, the center of activity. Down a side street I enter a 1919 church made of brick, with elaborate stained-glass windows, the home of the Herzstein Memorial Museum.

It's a quaint small-town museum, with displays of early life in Clayton. I see a country kitchen and artifacts from the days when trade caravans and homesteaders traveling along the Cimarrón Cutoff of the Santa Fe Trail passed near here, some of them stopping to settle. The town was founded in 1887 and became a major livestock-shipping center for herds from the Pecos Valley and Texas Panhandle — the air's musky scent today hints at the fact that it's still a haven to the cattle industry with five active feedlots.

A more startling depiction in the museum is in a hallway devoted to Thomas "Black Jack" Ketchum, an outlaw who was most noted for his death. Black-and-white photos show his 1901 execution in Clayton — a little too graphically, but it's history. There's a close-up of his head, which was severed clean off during the brutal hanging. The train robber's last words are recorded here too: "I'll be in hell before you start breakfast, boys."

I "head" out of town at dusk, allowing myself time to see the famed dinosaur footprints at nearby Clayton Lake State Park. Much has been written about them, as well as about the fishing at the lake, which holds the state record for a taken walleye: 32 inches and more than 16 pounds. That's tiny compared with the ancient wildlife here. More than 500 blackened indentations in sandstone step along a shelf above the lake, footprints left some 100 million years ago by a group of dinosaurs.

As I wait for night to fall, a few mule deer pass by, and then the sun sets and all is dark. Around 10 of us stand above the lake, the air smelling of prairie sage, and the stars so abundant the sky is golden. With a green laser beam, Terrell takes us on a tour, pointing out highlights visible with the naked eye. He shows us Polaris — the pole star, always marking the direction north.

"The sky is a compass, clock, calendar and time machine," he says. "When we look at stars, we're looking into the past." He points to the Andromeda Galaxy, a little more than two million light-years away. "The farthest thing you can see with the naked eye."

Next we move into the observatory, a small shed with a giant telescope at its heart. Terrell turns a crank to open the roof and then points the scope skyward. Tonight we see mostly stars through it. Whole galaxies become visible, like great wheels spinning through the universe with its billions of stars, crossed by dark bands of dust, gas and debris.

I can sense our place in the Milky Way Galaxy, sitting way out on one of its spiral arms. "From here, we have one of the best places to view the rest of the universe," says Terrell. And it's all possible from the little plains town of Clayton.

*Rabbit Ear Mountain's two striking mounds appeared as the first distinguishable features to Santa Fe Trail traffic crossing into New Mexico from Oklahoma and so became important landmarks.*

*Many of Clayton's downtown buildings hearken back to the early 1900s.*

*Dinosaur footprints near Clayton Lake State Park illustrate the presence of the grand creatures that once walked here.*

# ENCOUNTERS WITH THE NOTORIOUS IN PUERTO DE LUNA

WE AREN'T LOOKING FOR BILLY THE KID, HONEST. BUT IT SEEMS THAT EVERY COR-NER WE TURN IN PUERTO DE LUNA, WE FIND SIGNS OF HIS EXISTENCE.

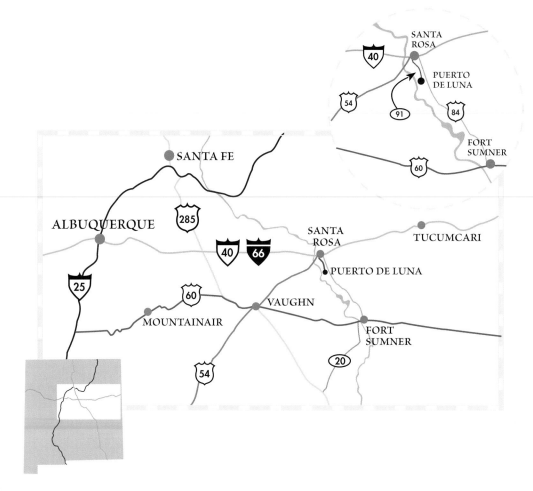

"My grandma used to hide Billy the Kid under her skirt," says Odilia Luna, while sitting on her porch in this northeastern New Mexico village 10 miles south of Santa Rosa. Our interest is definitely piqued by that statement about the famous 19th century outlaw, so we probe for more details.

*Living near the village church, Odilia Luna and her grandson Luis Campos take a break from their chile picking.*

"She hid him there from the cops, and he stayed still until they left."

Odilia paused from her fall chile picking to tell my mother and me this story. I feel blessed to have stumbled upon this woman, who, in her 70s or 80s, and recovering from a stroke, still makes her way amongst the chile rows, a plastic bag strung from her arm. She's joined by her 6-year-old grandson, Luis Campos.

My mother is often the key into doors like this. Gray-haired, with eyes as blue as the "bottomless" lakes in this part of the state, she inspires trust, and with a gentle curiosity, explores the depths of people's lives.

Today she talks with Odilia, and I get to sit back and listen to tales of this village. Though it's now a sleepy little place known for rich stories written by the contemporary author Rudolfo Anaya, it hasn't always been so.

Francisco Vázquez de Coronado spent time here some 450 years ago. Later, in the 1800s, the place was inhabited by a few thousand people, had five bars and hosted the notorious, including Billy the Kid, who sold stolen livestock in the area.

With strong roots here, Odilia knows her history. "I married into the Luna family," she says, referring to the Lunas for whom Puerto de Luna (Gate of the Moon) was named. She explains how the Lunas and other families migrated to this lush valley in the 1860s and used the Pecos River to irrigate corn, bean and chile fields.

Waving goodbye to Odilia and Luis, we head farther into the village, passing a noble stone structure surrounded by wildflowers that once was the Guadalupe County Court House. In the late 1800s, the village was the Guadalupe County seat, but when the railroad bypassed the town, its importance declined. Nearby, we find the local cathedral,

Nuestra Señora del Refugio (Our Lady of Refuge). Built in 1882, it has graceful lines and a shiny silver cupola.

Cruising along, we come to a sharp bend in the road, and my mother urges me to turn at an old pitched-roof adobe, marked by a sign reading "Alexander Grzelachowski House and Store." With a Polish name like that, who could refuse?

Here we meet Victor Flores, a quiet-spoken man who, along with his wife, Otilia, runs this historic museum next to their house. We're joined by their grandchildren, James and Felicia, who follow us into the structure that was once a store, saloon and residence. Through my mother's inquiry, we learn that Victor's father was born just down the road from this place and he used to come to the store to buy groceries. Of course, guess who else came here, too?

It's a ramshackle museum, with an old spinning wheel, a sagging bed and a pool table that probably saw some pretty feisty games. But the building, which is listed on the National Register of Historic Places, maintains its 1875 charm. You can almost hear the crusty cowboy boots tromping across the floors.

Out on the broad portal, Victor points to a hole in a post, where a bullet lodged when Billy the Kid allegedly shot a man through his hat "just for the hell of it."

"I myself took the bullet out when I was 10," says Victor. "My dad sold it for $5."

After giving a donation for museum upkeep, we say goodbye to Victor and the kids, and head farther down N.M. 91, hoping to find signs of other characters besides Billy. Coronado, maybe? In 1541, he and his troops camped here and likely schemed about where in the heck those Seven Cities of Gold could be. After traveling all the way up from what is now Mexico and Arizona, they were probably pretty discouraged with the state of their pocketbooks.

But they weren't defeated.

We come to a modern bridge and gaze down at the Pecos River that reflects an azure fall sky. It was right around here that Coronado gave the order to build a bridge — what some label the first bridge in the state. All we see is an old concrete slab off to the north.

Coronado and his troops crossed the bridge and headed east to what is now central Kansas and then returned, by then pretty well defeated by the lack of gold in these parts. We keep driving along the base of red cliffs, following the roaming Pecos, with little fields of corn and chile lining its banks. Finally, the road becomes dirt and so we turn around. From the south, Puerto de Luna appears pristine, with its cupola shining in the evening sun and smoke curling up from a lone chimney.

And Billy? Well, he's down there too, living an active life in a small town's memory.

*Some homes in Puerto de Luna hearken back to the 19th century.*

*In 1541 Francisco Vázquez de Coronado bridged the Pecos River here.*

# RATÓN HISTORIC DISTRICT:
## Many Stories and not a Single *Ratón* in Sight

THERE'S SOMETHING ABOUT NORTHEASTERN NEW MEXICO THAT INSPIRES STORYTELLING. MAYBE IT'S THE SLOW PACE, ALLOWING TIME FOR SUCH THINGS, OR MAYBE PEOPLE ARE JUST DRIVEN TO FILL THE LONG SILENCE AND EXPANSE OF THE GREAT PLAINS TO THE EAST.

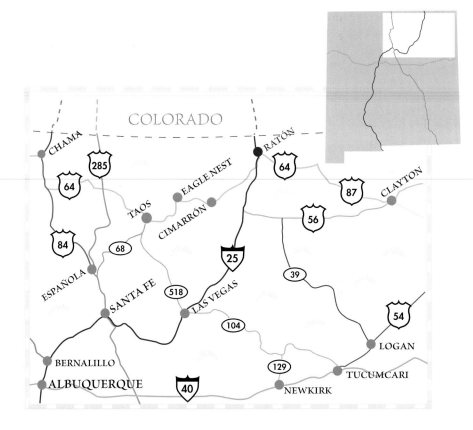

W hatever the reason, on a clear day, with winter still nipping at the heels of spring, we find a wealth of tales tucked away in the Ratón Downtown Historic District.

The district stretches across Ratón's main drag, but the undiscovered part lies a block east on First Street. There, Victorian storefronts face a still-operating 1903 Santa Fe Railway Depot. It's a street lined with antique shops, art galleries and a fun regional museum.

*The Raton train station offers a glimpse of Mission-style architecture common to many New Mexico stations.*

At the Ratón Museum we're greeted by the curator, Roger Sanchez. An open and modest man, he can elaborate on any of the many exhibits, from the tools of the railroad workers and fur traders of the 1880s when Ratón was founded, to relics of times even earlier and on into the present.

"In the 1700s, Spaniards camped at the foot of the mountain," he says, pointing toward the north. "During their stay, they were overrun by field mice. So they named it on the map as *Ratón* (mouse) Mountain — that's how the town got its name."

Fortunately, today, there's not a *ratón* in sight. There are, however, plenty more traveler stories. The Santa Fe Trail passes through the center of town and with it, tales of getting around the region. Ratón Pass proved an especially formidable obstacle in the 1800s.

"You were lucky if you made 800 yards a day over the pass," says Sanchez.

In 1877, the Atchison, Topeka & Santa Fe Railway arrived and conquered the pass, which constitutes the highest grade on the whole line from Chicago to Mexico. "It took four to five steam engines to pull a train over the top," says Sanchez. At that time, 400 machinists and mechanics worked in a roundhouse in Ratón, he adds, pointing out a period photo of the large building.

Next he tells us the story of coal — the commodity that brought more than 3,000 immigrants to the area. The museum holds safety signs in Spanish, Russian, Greek, Italian and Slavic, showing the variety of nationalities represented.

Swastika Coal Co. was one of the biggest employers in the late 1800s, its symbol emblazoned on a hotel in town, on signs and even on whiskey bottles that now rest empty here. "It's an ancient symbol," says Sanchez, "used long before Hitler took it and flipped it around."

Seven coal camps dotted the area, and the stories of tragedy and hardship are many. Mine explosions, oppressive company towns, it's all here, told through artifacts.

*Cathy Naylor helps take care of the Historic District, particularly her own Heirloom Shop.*

Other stories commingle with those: a footprint of *Tyrannosaurus Rex*, ancient fossils and rare *katsina* dolls made of bone, each with a wealth of lore attached to it.

Our minds full, my mother and I thank Sanchez and wander back out onto the street. With a Historic District Walking Tour map he gave us in hand, we note elaborately painted storefronts, some red brick, others bright silver, blue or maroon. We slip into the Heirloom Shop and meet Cathy Naylor and Hattie Sloan, who have had the place for 18 years. They buy area antiques, which have plenty of stories of their own. One of their favorite tales is of the 1906 Abourezk Building where their shop resides. Back in 1907, the building's namesake, a Lebanese family, ran a grocery store. When Mr. Abourezk died in 1930, his widow moved herself and her four children into the back of the store, where they lived for years. "With the store's earnings she sent her kids to college," Naylor says, her gaze passing around the room as though she were imagining it not only as a store, but also as a home. We, too, look around at the enchanting array of goods, from cut glass work, to antique tablecloths, to furniture.

Back on the street, we pass other shops and come to the pride of Ratón's citizens — the Old Pass Gallery. Funded by the Ratón Arts and Humanities Council, it sits within the 1910 Wells Fargo Express Building and carries works from more than 250 regional artists. The council is quite active in the area, sponsoring many events, including performances at the 1915 Historic Shuler Theater, a block to the east.

We make our way in that direction on Cook Street, appreciating the architecture of structures such as the 1918 Di Lisio Building with stained-glass windows, the neo-classical design of the 1917 U.S. Post Office and the swastikas on the 1929 Swastika Hotel.

This leads us to our accommodations for the night. The lovely Victorian building that houses Heart's Desire, a bed and breakfast, completes our historic experience. The boarding house was built in 1885 after the railroad came to Ratón. Proprietor Barbara Riley has restored it, adding many amenities. Most notable, rather than tromping out to an outhouse, guests use a well-equipped bath down the hall from the rooms.

Raised in nearby Roy and now a Ratón schoolteacher, Riley regales visitors with history. Her best account is of a train robbery out on the plains, for which her father served as the getaway man.

The eight-man team was never caught. Once the "take" was divided between them, they dispersed. "They never met again, but I have a treasure from the robbery," Riley says, showing off a pendant around her neck with a gold coin, her initials engraved on the back.

And so the stories go. That night we slept among them, the voices of times past echoing in our dreams.

Top: *In the center of the Ratón Downtown Historic District, enchanting buildings, many from the 1800s, provide a fun atmosphere for strolling.*

Bottom: *Proprietor Barbara Riley serves a delicious breakfast as well as plenty of tasty tales at Heart's Desire bed and breakfast.*

# ROCIADA: Land Sprinkled With Dew

"DID YOU SEE THOSE BUGS?" I ASK MY MOTHER.
"WHAT BUGS?" SHE REPLIES.
"HUGE, TRUCK-SIZE BUGS." I BACK UP THE CAR AND THERE THEY ARE, NEXT TO THE ROAD, NEARLY CRAWLING OVER US.
"OH," SHE SAYS. "THOSE BUGS."

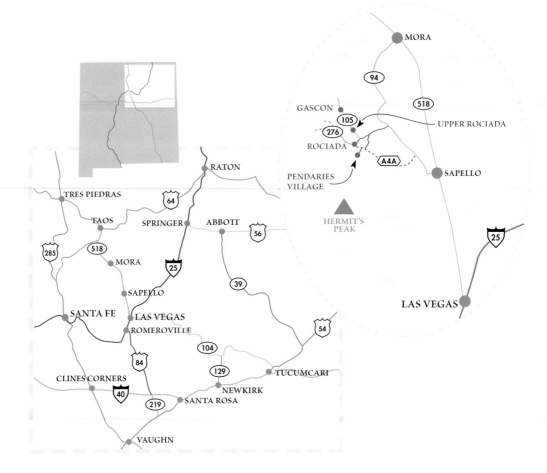

*A*nd thus begins our journey to the village of Rociada on the edge of the Pecos Wilderness in northeastern New Mexico. On this fall day, with clouds shuffling among the hills, we discover it's a place of many mysteries.

The first we solve quickly. The bugs. They're the inventive creation of Paul Dolloff, an artist with a face burned red from welding and a passion for junk. He spends his free time perusing junkyards, bringing home all manner of discarded parts. Then he assembles them into lizards, penguins, birds, porcupines, turtles and, most notably, the creepier creations — bugs. "I try to find parts that look like what I'm trying to make," he says. "Motorcycle gas tanks work especially well."

*In his studio, Paul Dolloff works on one of the oversized bugs he's renowned for making.*

He and his wife, Barbara Marigold, live in a cozy home with a striking view of 10,260-foot-high Hermit's Peak. She makes weavings, tapestries and rugs in brilliant gold, green and azure, also, at times, using discarded materials. Ties for men are one of her favorite creations. "Men think it's great to do anything with ties — except wear them," she says. Both artists sell their work at Marigold Arts on Canyon Road in Santa Fe.

Farther down the road we see the next mystery. Along the edge of the valley is a warehouse-size building, restored in pale stucco. It sits near Pendaries Village, a community of homes gathered around an 18-hole golf course with fairways that snake up into the pine-covered hills. One resident of Pendaries, Pat Patrick, volunteers to show us around. He's a native of Texas who retired here 10 years ago and doesn't like to leave. "It's a collection of really neat homes and people," he says of Pendaries.

Deeply interested in the region's history, he fills us in, the story accentuated by his Texas drawl. The building is an 1876 gristmill, built by Frenchman Jean Pendaries, who settled in this valley and ranched some 4,000 acres here. The mill has an 18-foot-high water wheel and once was the center of the valley's business and social scene. "It stopped grinding grain in the 1930s," Pat says. Next to it, also from the late 1800s, is the well-restored ranch commissary, which is now a private home.

Deeper into the valley, we come to the village itself — Rociada, the most poetic name in the state to my ear. It's a classic northern New Mexico village with adobe homes clustered around the Santo Niño Church. Just off the plaza is the home of James and Barbara Atencio.

*Barbara and James Atencio and their grand-daughter Allison Atencio live in Rociada.*

A quiet man with an open face, James taught in Las Vegas and drove a school bus for years, but his passion is ranching in this valley, and he still does it. "My family came here in the 1850s," he says as we sit in his living room, a fire crackling in the woodstove. His ancestors used to graze sheep and cattle across the mountains in the Río Grande Valley. "They looked over the top one day and decided to move here," he says.

The valley's beauty likely drew them. Set below 10,906-foot-high Spring Mountain, it's made up of broad meadows and protected on all sides by pine-covered hills. The name Rociada describes it best. "It means 'sprinkled with dew,'" says James. "It's always wet. Even in the drought, it's green."

He talks of the early years in the village and smiles when he speaks of his grandfather, who used to train horses and ride them in the high country above us. In one story, his grandfather's horse spooked coming off Gascon Point and bucked all the way down. "He used to say to me, 'Don't do that!' — As if I ever would," James says with a fond laugh. "Granddad even rode a palomino to the state fair," he adds, pointing to the southwest toward Albuquerque, a trip of more than 100 miles. "He won third place."

We wave goodbye to the Atencios and make our way to Upper Rociada, a smaller village set at 8,000 feet. It's tucked below the gracefully arching Gascon Point that James spoke of, which was named for Frenchman Jean Pendaries' homeland Gascony in France. Upper Rociada is a cluster of pitched, tin-roofed homes surrounding the sturdy, adobe-colored San José Church.

As we leave the village, we pass a sign along the road that reads *"Vaqueros de las Sierras"* — Cowboys of the Mountains. Here, set below the towering Gascon Point, I can imagine such cowboys, much like James and his grandfather, mythic characters who dwell in a place with truck-sized bugs and a mysterious dew that keeps grass forever green.

*In the nearby Sapello Valley, an old mill sits below Hermit's Peak.*

*En route to Rociada, a village church shines golden in the evening light.*

# Southeast

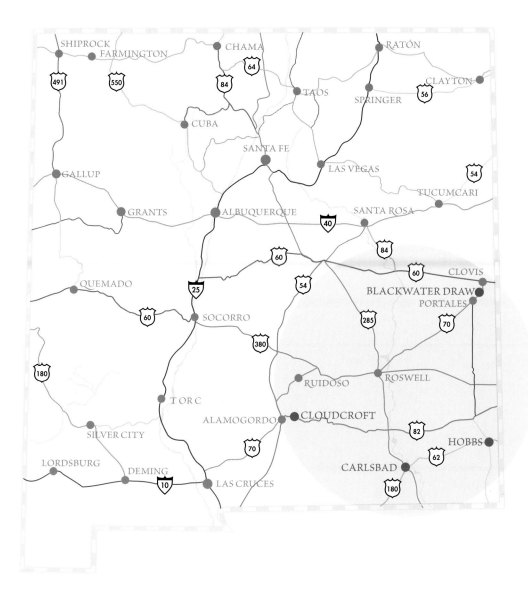

## LISTENING TO BONES: A Journey through Blackwater Draw

THIS IS THE TALE OF A HEROIC ARCHAEOLOGICAL SITE. FROM THE FIRST FINDING OF SOME TEETH BURIED DEEP IN THE SAND IN EASTERN NEW MEXICO NEAR PORTALES, BLACKWATER DRAW HAS STRUGGLED TO BE RECOGNIZED FOR WHAT IT IS: ONE OF THE MOST IMPORTANT PALEO-INDIAN SITES IN THE AMERICAS.

*Now a small canyon, Blackwater Draw was once a sand and gravel mine.*

I t has endured battle after battle against a formidable foe, emerging to be what it is today. Just what is it? I set out with my mother, who studied archaeology in college, to find out.

We make our way east across plains that seem to stretch forever, a place where the highest landmark is a train that gradually creeps upon us on a straight horizon and then, just as slowly, disappears. Suddenly, the land drops away into a canyon called Backwater Draw. The site's tireless advocate, Joanne Dickenson, greets us. She's a hearty woman with thousands of years of history in her head and a willing enthusiasm to relate it.

She explains that in 1929, a Boy Scout found a spear point and some American mammoth teeth here and sent them to the Smithsonian Institution in Washington, D.C. Thus began the scientific interest in the place, which has continued for years.

The land immediately shows signs of this site's heroic journey. The draw was dug out of the plains not by delicate archaeologists carefully brushing away sand with toothbrushes, as one might hope. Instead, dirt was dug and hauled away with backhoes and front-end loaders, dredgers and dump trucks.

This once was a sand and gravel mine.

We head down into the pit, where elm trees and wild grasses now grow. Joanne explains that an archaeologist working under Dr. Edgar Howard in 1936 found spear points set in relation to American mammoth bones. Though this might seem like no big deal today, it was and still is important.

"These were the first and earliest mammoth bones discovered in association with human tools," Joanne says. "Before that no one knew how long people had been in the New World." The bones helped lock in time human habitation here, dating to nearly 12,000 years ago.

Over time, the remains of at least 20 species of animals — as well as mammoth — surfaced. It once was a rich spring, drawing saber-toothed cat, dire wolf, extinct Bison, pre-Columbian horse and animals that I never knew walked this continent such as camel and giant sloth.

*Eastern New Mexico University graduate student Tori Myers excavates bones in the Interpretive Center.*

And still the mining continued.

Though some earlier attempts were made to protect the site, not until 1962 did the government take action, and even then it took years to stop the mining. "We're still fighting the effects of it," says Joanne, pointing to piles of dirt scattered across the draw. "All the hills you see are left from it."

We climb to higher ground and step into a large metal building, the Interpretive Center, and there the true beauty of the site becomes apparent. Thousands of bones stretch before us in amazing configurations.

Tori Myers, an Eastern New Mexico University graduate student, works from her knees on the dark earth. "I'm exposing as much as possible but still leaving the bones in place," she says.

At this moment, Tori brushes away dirt from a female bison skeleton with something amazing attached. Tucked within her elaborate spine-and-ribs bone structure is a tiny replica of herself — the skeleton of a baby. "She either died while pregnant or while giving birth," Tori says. "This is one of the reasons we don't want to take the bones away, because here, within a 5-foot space, there's a whole story."

Through viewing the "bone bed," we get a sense of the distinct strata, from the times before humans, up into the Clovis period and the later Folsom, and even to more modern times when tribes such as the Apache roamed here. "The stratigraphic record is a world-renowned reference point for Paleo-Indian studies," says Joanne.

Leaving the shelter of that cavelike building, we make our way deeper into this gash in the earth. At one point Joanne stops fast in her tracks. "That's the mammoth kill site," she says, pointing to a grove of cottonwoods. Her eyes sparkle with the excitement of this place where five skeletons of the huge, hairy elephant-like mammoth were found, along with almost 2,000 artifacts.

We climb out of the draw onto the dry and flat plains, where we travel east. Near the town of Portales, we stop in at the Blackwater Draw Museum, hoping it will help us further piece together the history.

The museum holds exhibits that are a bit of a letdown after what we saw "in the field." I had imagined seeing the bones of a giant mammoth pieced together, towering over us. But as I recall, this is a story of struggle. A majority of the bones went on to larger venues, such as the University of Pennsylvania and the Texas Memorial Museum.

We see a replica of the head of a giant mammoth, created by graduate students who also made most of the displays. Painted dioramas help us visualize what the flora and fauna were like. What's most impressive is the assortment of spear points set in a historical timeline.

I look at the delicate artistry of a point such as the Clovis or Folsom, and imagine that someone chipped out each little notch more than 10,000 years ago.

Back out in the eastern New Mexico brightness, I ask my mother what she thought of it all. Her answer is simple: "Most digs," she says, "are not that concise." And I reflect, maybe that's what happens when you fight every moment to exist. The dross slips away, leaving the true essence.

*Grain silos such as these form poetic landmarks at sunset in this flat land.*

*Bones of a young mammoth's feet give a sense of the grandeur of the animals that once walked this land.*

## CHRISTMAS ON THE PECOS:
### River of Lights

I FLOAT AT NIGHT ON CALM WATER, MY SENSES HEIGHTENED BY THE DARKNESS. A CHILD'S LAUGHTER DRIFTS BY AND THE SCENT OF SUGAR COOKIES FILLS THE AIR, WHILE A COOL CHIHUAHUAN DESERT BREEZE BRUSHES MY CHEEKS.

S uddenly, the song "Feliz Navidad" lilts across the inky surface and lights appear, their reflections wavering — red, blue, green and gold.

This is Christmas on the Pecos, an event praised by A&E Network as one of the Top 10 Small Town Winter Events in the United States, yet still a quiet and calm experience that befits the season. It's a generous offering of beauty by some 125 homeown-ers — artists really — who paint the night with light.

Nestled snugly in a pontoon boat with a blanket to keep me warm, I'm among 20 passengers cruising the Pecos River past sloping backyards of expansive homes. We see oversized gold stars adorning a tree, Santa and elves lounging on a beach, and a white-lit forest with bears and raccoons peeking through the branches. In the boat, kids crane their necks to look in all directions, while our captain, Dale Balzano, shares Carlsbad Christmas lore.

*The Pecos River Village welcomes visitors with its Christmas cheer.*

This is the 17th year that homeowners along the Pecos have decorated their backyards, he says. During the season, he makes more than 200 trips on this one-mile stretch. "I could tell you what lightbulb's out," he chuckles. In all, approximately 16,000 people take this ride throughout the holidays. It's a different experience from the commercial tours that some larger cities hold, Dale explains. "Every homeowner puts his or her heart into creating something — adding their own touch."

These touches range across the spectrum of experience. We pass a dog wearing a Santa hat, a red Ferris wheel run by a snowman, reindeer grazing amongst zigzag trees, a water dragon, a spinning carousel, and the words "God Bless You" branding the darkness with white. All cast down on the water surrounding us, their colors shimmering and blending with our motion, becoming an impressionistic blur. I have to close my eyes to return to reality.

Sated with light and color, I leave the river, the song "White Christmas" still playing in

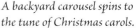
*A backyard carousel spins to the tune of Christmas carols.*

my head. The sensuous ride is just part of the celebration here. Starting Thanksgiving weekend, the season also includes a Calico Christmas Arts and Crafts Show — a great place to buy gifts — and a Holiday Stroll, when locals and visitors shop late on the town's decorated main street. These events culminate with an electric-light parade, in which illuminated floats cruise through town.

I head to the home of Michael and Josephine Calvani, who live along the river. Mike is co-chair of the committee that puts on the event, though he emphasizes that it's a community effort led by the Carlsbad Chamber of Commerce and local volunteers. He inherited his interest in holiday decorating from his parents. "My mother and father were really into Christmas," he says.

While taking me across his sloping lawn toward the river, he tells more about the experience of putting up the displays. "We're seeing year after year the quality gets better," he says. Some homeowners put up so many lights that they "blow out" their electricity, he adds with a laugh. "Several have run extra power."

He waves his arm across the lights in front of us. "When you're an isolated community in the middle of the desert and you're able to do something like this, something you can't even see in a bigger city, it really takes on meaning."

At the edge of the water stands the Santa-and-elves beach scene we passed earlier, created with a lightness of spirit that so emanates from Mike. A boat floats by, the passengers barely visible across the water, but on their faces, even in the dark, I can see what I experienced on the trip — the feeling that this season celebrates: wondrous joy.

Christmas on the Pecos runs nightly, Thanksgiving through New Year's Eve, except for Christmas Eve.

*Sunset on the Pecos River previews the show to come.*

*During the boat ride, lights and their reflections paint a fairytale world.*

# AMBLING BACK TO THE OLD WEST IN CLOUDCROFT

"MY DAD TOLD ME IT WOULD TAKE A COUPLE OF YEARS TO LEARN HOW TO MOSEY. HE COACHED ME BEFORE I CAME HERE," SAYS GREG STONER, WHO IS TENDING BAR AT THE LODGE AT CLOUDCROFT.

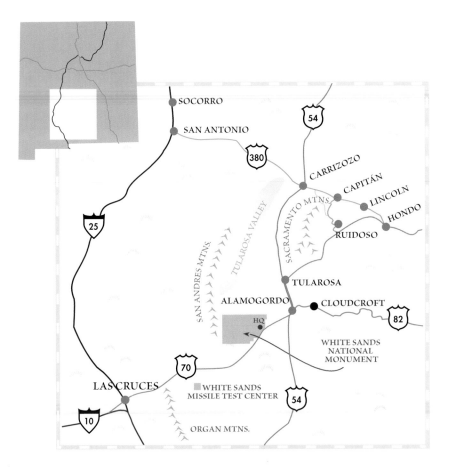

SOCORRO

SAN ANTONIO

54

380

CARRIZOZO

CAPITÁN

LINCOLN

SACRAMENTO MTNS.

HONDO

25

RUIDOSO

TULAROSA VALLEY

SAN ANDRES MTNS.

TULAROSA

ALAMOGORDO

CLOUDCROFT

HQ

82

WHITE SANDS
NATIONAL
MONUMENT

70

LAS CRUCES

WHITE SANDS
MISSILE TEST CENTER

54

10

ORGAN MTNS.

My mother and I listen intently to this adventurous young man who escaped a fast-paced modern life in California in order to move here.

"It's priceless to be stressless," he adds.

We've sidled up to the bar to have a libation before heading into a weekend of celebration of the same notions that Greg is promoting and that seem to be the philosophy of this mountain town. Cloudcroft's Western Heritage Days celebrate an attitude that's mostly lost today: the simple life of the pioneers of this land.

*Diana Holder displays her Mississippi mud pie before the auction. "I love it here," she says of Cloudcroft. "What's not to love, the weather, the people, the mountains."*

Our first stop is Zenith Park, where in an open field surrounded by cottonwood trees we settle onto picnic benches with about 50 locals and visitors to eat barbecue brisket and baked potatoes. While we savor the meal, a microphone buzzes and auctioneer Carl Wood welcomes us to the pie auction.

He holds up a delectable creation — a Mississippi mud pie baked by Diana Holder. It's a gooey looking concoction of walnuts and marshmallows that even from a distance smells of its main ingredient: chocolate. The auctioneer starts the bidding at $200, but when there are no takers, he smiles sheepishly.

"Maybe I started a little high," he says. "How about five?" A hand shoots up. The bidding closes at $20.

"Sold!"

And thus the auction goes, buttermilk pumpkin pecan pie, blueberry cheesecake, cinnamon-apple pie. One woman bids up to $45 and gets her pick of the remaining pies, while my mother buys one and donates it straight back to sell again, with a wink at me, knowing the temptation of having such a delicacy in our hotel room the whole night.

Once the pies are gone, the crowd makes its way to an open-air pavilion nearby. We follow, arriving just in time to hear them boo a villain and then cheer enthusiastically for

*At dusk, The Lodge at Cloudcroft shines in the ponderosa pines.*

a hero. The Cloudcroft Light Opera Company's production of *The Cowhand Christmas Carol* is all that a melodrama should be, with love and shady real-estate deals, and kids running up to the stage to throw popcorn.

By night's end, our throats weary from yelling, we head back to The Lodge at Cloudcroft. It's the reason the town exists at all. In the late 1800s, the El Paso and Northeastern Railroad ran a train track up into these mountains to haul away trestle timber. They built The Lodge, which later burned. But in 1911, it was replaced by this hotel, an enchanting relic with a Victorian tower, plush red-velvet interior and views out across the cloudlike White Sands National Monument some 4,500 feet below. And yet it's modern too, with a 9-hole Scottish-style golf course, a spa and a gourmet restaurant.

After a good night's sleep, we head over to Burro Avenue and get a sense of this quaint town. It has an Old West feel with wooden storefronts and even a hitching post to tie up your horse. One of the highest towns in the state, it sits at 8,650 feet and has about 750 inhabitants, though that number triples in summer.

The town grew up as a vacation village around The Lodge, but many visitors have come to stay, spending their time shopping along the boardwalk and hiking the mountains. Says one of them, echoing our bartender friend: "You won't see too many clocks in this town. Nobody cares about time."

Certainly today, time has swung back. Nearby, the Sacramento Mountains Historical Museum is lively with Old West activity. A Las Cruces blacksmith hammers metal over an anvil, while a Corona sheep grower spins wool on a traditional Saxony wheel. A mountain man demonstrates how to load a flint rifle, and a homesteader shows how to make chuckwagon biscuits. Meanwhile, a sheriff roams about, searching for wayward kids to throw in jail, and a guitar duo plays folk songs. With the brilliant summer light shining, these olden days take on a romantic feel.

We meet up with James and Jamey Sevier, a father and daughter from Artesia dressed in fringed buckskin who have attended the celebration for the past three years. Jamey sums up the experience well.

"It's great gettin' to see all the old-timey stuff," Jamey says. "That way we don't ever forget what happened in the past, what our heritage is."

They especially look forward to the street dance planned for tonight, but our interest turns to the missing piece of this puzzle of yesteryear. We find it at Zenith Park, where a group of Mescalero Apache dancers have gathered to do a Round Dance — a friendship dance.

A group of Boy Scouts spreads out in a circle with the dancers, stepping and twirling to drumbeats. The sound echoes through the canyon and seems to bounce across time with an age-old message: The quiet rhythm of a simple and relaxed life doesn't rely on when you live, or even where you live, but on what you truly desire.

*Nestled in the pines, Cloudcroft offers views of White Sands National Monument, some 4,500 feet lower in elevation.*

*Franklyn Red Elk, one of the Mescalero Apache dancers, prepares for the Eagle Dance.*

65

## HOBBS:
## Land of Big
## Belt Buckles

"THERE ARE MORE BIG BELT BUCKLES HERE THAN ANYWHERE ELSE IN THE WORLD."

THAT CLAIM, OFTEN MADE BY RESIDENTS OF HOBBS, IS NOT ABOUT FASHION. IT'S ABOUT SPORTS.

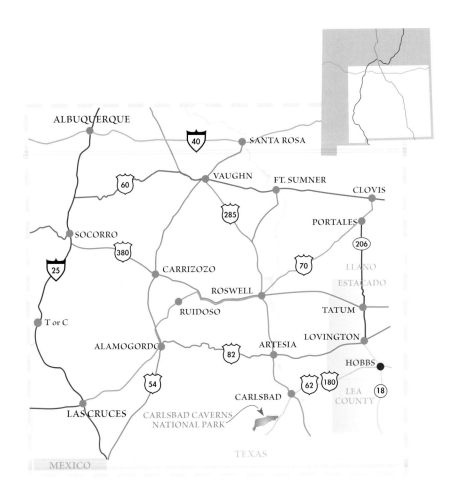

I n fact, the small southeastern New Mexico oil town perched near the border of Texas is home to more champion cowboys than anywhere on the globe, each with his or her own trophy belt buckle to prove it.

It's no accident, my mother and I learn as we head down there one wildly atmospheric day, battling our way through hail showers that move like dusky curtains across miles of flat prairie. This land and its people live and breathe ranching and the cowboy life.

*With his cowboy hat, country drawl and years of work on horseback, sculptor Curtis Fort epitomizes a Lea County cowboy.*

We're set to meet one of its best examples. A notable bronze sculptor and an old family friend, Curtis Fort, greets us at the Western Heritage Museum & Lea County Cowboy Hall of Fame. He stands in the lobby wearing knee-high boots and a black broad-brimmed hat, ready to show us around.

"These plains were like an ocean," he says, immediately setting the tone of Lea County and bringing a sense of mystery to it. First let me explain that Curtis is most known for the stories his bronze sculptures tell, gritty tales of cowboying in the late 1800s and early 1900s, fed by his own experience growing up on a ranch and years of work at such renowned and vast operations as the Vermejo Park and Bell ranches.

"There were lakes but nobody knew it, so travelers went around the area. It's a tough old place," he says of this land named the *Llano Estacado*, or Staked Plains, for reasons that many still speculate upon and debate. "When I ride, sometimes there's not a hill, not a landmark. If a horse was to buck you off and you hit your head, you wouldn't know what direction you were going."

Curtis Fort's grandparents lived in a dugout here once, which to my amazement, was how everyone lived when the area was first settled. "There were no trees," says Lisa Seed, the director of the Cowboy Hall of Fame, who joins us on the tour. "Nothing to build with. So

*Wildflowers accentuate the horizon's flatness in a land where no natural water flows, so few, if any, trees grow.*

you had to live underground."

She stands back and shakes her head as though still awed by this place where she grew up. "Every tree that's here was planted by somebody."

It's remarkable that a town without a river nor natural running water today boasts broad, tree-lined avenues and a complete but some-what non-descript business district. The town's existence relies on water pumped up from the Ogalala Aquifer.

We continue meandering through the history of this land defined by great vastness, Curtis talking with his rich cowboy drawl. We see tributes to the 12 Professional Rodeo Cow-boys Association (PRCA) champions, as well as others who have contributed to the region. There's a replica of a chuckwagon and a Plains Indian teepee. But for me, the most interesting part is what distinctly resonates with the *Llano Estacado* — ranch history.

"Cowboying is the same now as 100 years ago," Curtis says. "It still takes a guy or gal on horseback." He points to a map that shows how, back in the early 1900s, the area was split up between only a handful of ranches. The Jal, San Simon, Hat and a few other spreads each encompassed hundreds of square miles of unfenced land where ranchers grazed thousands of cows.

In the museum's gallery we pass in front of one of the Curtis bronzes situated among many other Western art pieces. *The Night Horse* is a sturdy quarter horse, stand-ing tall with a saddle.

"Back in the open range days, you needed a horse saddled at night," Curtis explains. "You had two-hour guard duty, staying with the herd. You maybe had the midnight to 2 (a.m.) shift."

He touches a hoof. "So that's why he's hobbled, with a bridle over the saddle horn." Such stories aren't always obvious. They can be subtle, lying hidden below the surface, as is the most catalytic part of the Hobbs story.

In the museum we come to an illustrated exhibit. We learn that this quiet agrarian community,

*The ubiquitous oil wells in the region even pump away in backyards in the middle of Hobbs.*

founded in 1907 by James Isaac Hobbs, busted open in 1928 when the Midwest Refinery Co. (now Amoco) struck oil. Seven hundred barrels of "black gold" snaked to the surface each day, turning the town into an oil camp with shacks and tents. They poured crude on the main street to settle the dust.

Subsequent years, including those of the Great Depression, created a jagged boom-and-bust timeline for the city, but it continued to grow and produce oil. Today, you can hardly cast your gaze in any direction without seeing a well.

We note this as we leave the museum and say goodbye to Curtis, who heads back home to Tatum. At one point we come across a well seesawing away in what appears to be someone's backyard.

"I would paint mine blue," says my mom, dreaming that she might have one of her very own.

Not far from the museum, we see the city's newest catalyst — a casino and horseracing track, Black Gold Casino at Zia Park. Later, the president of the chamber of commerce, Ray Battaglini, answers a question everyone seems to ask: Why a racetrack, in Hobbs?

"Horseracing is now the fastest growing spectator sport in the country," he says, explaining that Hobbs draws from the West Texas market. With a racetrack comes the ability to offer gambling, which feeds the racing purses. "A lot of breeders are coming here to raise horses now," he says.

And so, I guess, that's Hobbs most modern version of the horseman, still astride a steed, but now traveling 45 mph across the *Llano Estacado*. But sadly, no big belt buckle.

# Southwest

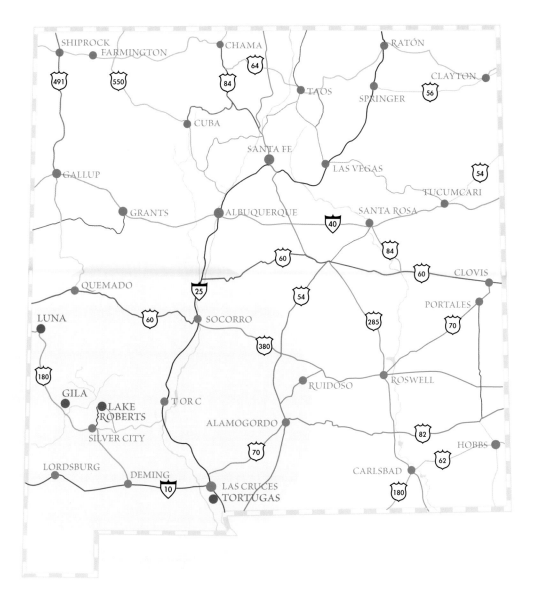

# THE WILD WORLD OF GILA

THE VILLAGE OF GILA IS NOT EXACTLY A HOT DESTINATION SPOT — NO FRILLY RESORTS, NO GLITZY MALLS WHERE POWER-SHOPPERS CAN WEAR THEIR PLASTIC THIN. AND YET, THE ADVENTUROUS TRAVELER WILL FIND PLENTY TO DO HERE, WITH THE ADDED BONUS OF A LIVELY RURAL CULTURE.

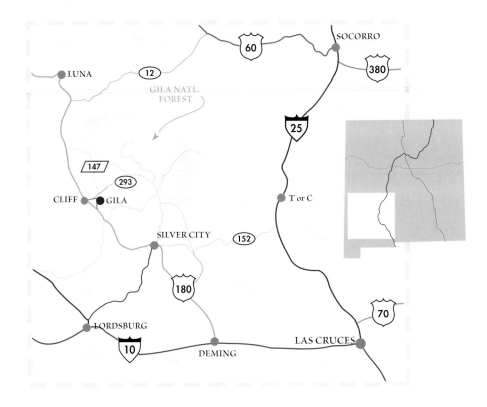

*Valley Market and Valley Hardware form the center of the community, places where people can stock up on necessities and meet up with friends.*

$G$ila sits on the edge of the Gila National Forest's 3.3 million acres and is most known as a jumping off point for some of its more rugged and obscure trails. But there are other high points as well: a stunning riparian preserve, ranch-style horseback riding trips and a couple of peaceful inns where visitors can soak in the quiet.

Fortunately, we hit this sleepy town on a Thursday coffee-in-the-park day for locals. David Gierke welcomes us to a picnic table where Gila old-timers and new-timers alike sip java and, on this particular morning, pass around photos of David's van, which was crushed into the ground by a falling cottonwood tree.

If you've ever lived in a small town like Gila, you'll know that such down-home events often eclipse the national news. They draw people together to stand and ponder, nod their heads and hem and haw over the awesome force that surrounds them and affects their daily lives — nature.

Such hemming and hawing has likely gone on for centuries in this valley. Its first noted residents were the Salado people, who hunted and fished the area between 1325 and 1475 and left behind ruins known as *Kwilleylekia*, which unfortunately are off-limits to visitors.

After the Saladoans, farmers settled the valley, including a Mormon group known as the Clarks in 1865. An ancestor of the group, Robert Clark, grew up in Gila and has followed the area's history over the years. He tells of how, in the late 1800s, the L-C Ranch laid hold to much of the land. "They claimed they ran cattle from the Canada border to the Mexican border," says Clark. This might be less an exaggeration than it sounds since back then most of the land was unfenced.

After the owners of the L-C died, the land slowly dispersed again, but in the mid-1950s the Pacific Western Land and Cattle Co. began buying up farms. "They bought the land gradually for the water rights," says Clark. Indeed, the Pacific Western was owned by Phelps

73

Jo Dee Birch, owner of Valley Market, grew up in Gila and is part of the Clark family, Mormons who came to the valley in 1865.

Dodge Mining Co., which used the water in their Tyrone copper mine.

Clark's daughter, Jo Dee Birch, has witnessed the more recent changes in the valley. "There used to be a lot of farmers when I was a kid," she says, "but now there are only a few."

Jo Dee and her husband, Robby Birch, own Valley Market at the center of town. With video rentals and a full line of groceries, it's the Wal-Mart of the area, as well as the meeting place for locals (besides the post office). The community is so quiet it seems as though little could have changed throughout the years, but Jo Dee sees things differently. "About 10 years ago I knew everybody," she says. "But since then a lot of people moved from back East and overseas."

Next, we head toward the mountains in search of the Nature Conservancy's Gila Riparian Preserve, a designation that protects 10 miles of river. We come to N.M. 293 and drive right up to the edge of the wilderness, where rocky crags jut up into a sky darkening fast with storm clouds.

A jaunt through a campground takes us to the preserve. This isn't an established place with a visitor center and designated trails. Instead, it's a wild place of bushy cottonwoods, brambles and loose river stones. We make our way to the bank of Mogollón Creek and sit near the water, watching trout rise to the surface and swallows flit under a canopy of cottonwoods.

A naturalist's paradise, this waterway flows into the Gila River, one of the last free-flowing rivers of the West. It's home to native desert fish that have disappeared from many other Southwestern rivers, as well as 40 endangered plant and animal species.

From the preserve we strike out toward the northwest on one of New Mexico's loveliest graded dirt roads. Forest Service Road 147, also known as Sacaton Road, meanders along the most unexplored region at the base of the Gila Wilderness. It leads past some excellent trailheads (I recommend the Rain Creek Trail No. 189) and across broad plains where cattle graze, backdropped by the incredible craggy beauty of the Gila.

Now, the storm that has been building comes full force, with blue and purple clouds roiling and shifting above our heads. Lightning bolts charge the sky, chasing us back to the more civilized world of U.S. 180.

*Gila is surrounded by the Chihuahuan Desert, which is backed by the pristine blue of the Gila Wilderness.*

*Set on the edge of the Gila Wilderness, the Gila Riparian Preserve protects 10 miles of river, a naturalist's paradise.*

## HUMMINGBIRD SAFARI AT LAKE ROBERTS

ZOOM . . . ZOOM. THAT'S THE SOUND I HEAR WHILE STANDING IN A PARKING LOT AT LAKE ROBERTS IN SOUTHERN NEW MEXICO. ALONG WITH THE SOUND COMES A RUSH OF AIR TICKLING MY EARS. I'M HERE STALKING A WILDLIFE SPECIMEN OF THE MINUTEST KIND.

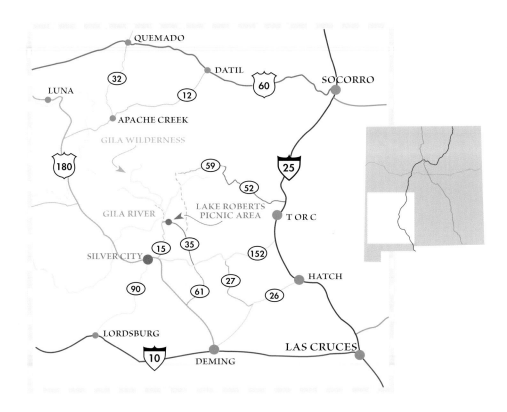

QUEMADO

DATIL

LUNA

32

12

60

SOCORRO

APACHE CREEK

GILA WILDERNESS

180

59

25

52

GILA RIVER

LAKE ROBERTS
PICNIC AREA

T OR C

SILVER CITY

15

35

152

HATCH

90

61

27

26

LORDSBURG

10

DEMING

LAS CRUCES

*The town's namesake, Lake Roberts, offers canoeing, boating and fishing for catfish and trout.*

I t weighs as little as a penny and yet is strong enough to fly all the way from here to Alaska. Its feathers can be blindingly bright: iridescent green, cobalt or magenta. And its names feed the imagination: calliope, rufous, broad-tailed, black-chinned — what else could be so wondrous but hummingbirds?

It's a warm day in this little village named for a lake surrounded by ponderosa-studded hills, which were once home to the Mimbres tribes. Today, the area holds a smattering of houses and businesses in a long canyon cut by Sapello Creek with the Gila and Mimbres rivers flowing nearby. It's a place where nature dominates, mainly in the form of the tiniest of birds.

Their presence here is huge, which I first note when I stop in at Grey Feathers Lodge. With a broad porch, this place provides a perfect start for my wildlife safari. The dining room is lined with picture windows looking out on many feeders, so I can see the birds through the glass as they drink inches away, their little throats swallowing and wings flapping so fast they're invisible.

Linda Galloway — who owns the lodge with her husband Jim — believes the area is so blessed with birds because of the attitude here: "They get a sense of where it's really safe," she says. At the front entrance of the Grey Feathers, the Galloways list sightings: nine varieties of hummingbirds, bald eagles, sapsuckers, Montezuma quail, osprey and the rarer purple martin, to name a few.

Besides having such a welcoming attitude toward birds, Lake Roberts has an ideal location to attract them. It sits within the 3.3 million-acre Gila National Forest and is on a migratory route directed by the Rocky Mountains. All the flowing water provides a rich habitat as well.

Farther up the canyon I come to the town's namesake: Lake Roberts. It's a placid, blue lake, a good place to canoe, boat and fish for bluegill, bass, catfish and trout. Unfortunately,

due to a parasite in the water, swimming is discouraged. Visitors can rent boats and stock up on licenses, baked beans and fresh eggs at the Lake Roberts General Store, a classic small-town spot, with a line of hummingbird feeders out front. Zoom . . . Zoom.

Continuing on my expedition, I pull into the driveway of a sweet little whitewashed home whose front is, of course, filled with feeders, the air abuzz with birds zooming by. Behind the house are some canvas booths where vendors sell pottery, pine furniture and yummy smelling banana-nut muffins. Farther along, Joan Day-Martin holds a hummingbird in her palm.

This is the Hummingbirds of New Mexico Festival, the highlight of which I see now, as Joan prepares to band the bird. The task seems more impossible than taming a rhino to me. The creature is so fragile and wild, but Joan has banded over 12,000 of them so she obviously knows how. With assistants helping, she weighs and measures the creature and then applies a tiny metal bracelet etched with numbers to its ankle. To show her solidarity, Joan wears a larger version on her own ankle.

"I'm identified," she jokes. "If I come back, we'll know what year I first came here."

That's the point of this, to keep track of the "population dynamics," find out how long the birds live, how hardy they are and where they go. Joan is one of only 125 people in the world permitted by the U.S. Fish and Wildlife Service to do this work. She explains that the banding helps answer many questions, such as where the birds migrate and how long they live. It was once thought that they lived only two years. "The oldest bird we've found through banding is 12," she says.

When the work is done, she holds the lovely creature up to my ear. The bird stays completely still while I listen to its heartbeat, which sounds like rushing water. Then, gently, Joan sets it on my palm, where I can barely feel its weight. It sits still for moments, long enough for me to consider what makes these birds so fascinating. They fly not only forward but also straight up and down, sideways and backwards, beating their wings some 50 times per second and traveling up to 35 mph.

And yet here it sits, so light I can only sense it, so fragile . . . well, I don't even like to think of all the ways it could be harmed. These unique creatures possess an equal balance of what could be the most coveted qualities: strength and delicacy. In a rush of feathers, it zooms away. I rub my palm fondly, wondering if I'll ever wash it again.

*At the Lake Roberts General Store locals and visitors stock up on baked beans, corn starch and regional books.*

# AIMING FOR THE MOON IN LUNA

IT SEEMS THAT SUCCESSFUL PEOPLE OFTEN ACCOMPLISH WHATEVER THEY TRULY IMAGINE. TOWNS ARE NO DIFFERENT, OR SO I DISCOVER ON A JOURNEY TO EXPERIENCE WHAT THE TOWN OF LUNA HAS COINED "THE WORLD'S BIGGEST SMALL TOWN RODEO."

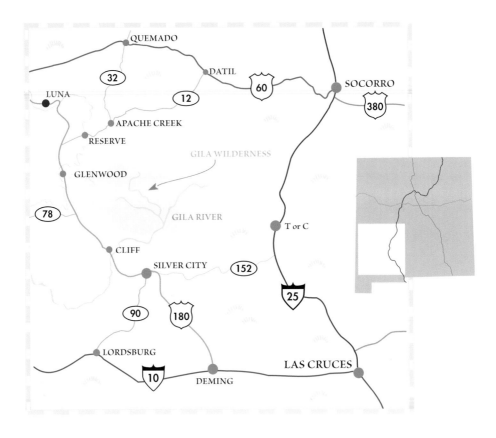

E arly on a bright July day I pull into a lush valley carved by the San Francisco River and get my first glimpse of Luna. It's but a whisper of a town on New Mexico's south-western border. The commu-nity's main street is studded with a few historic homes, one belonging to Carol and Joe Laney.

*On Pioneer Day, Joe and Carol Laney celebrate their Mormon ancestors, who settled Luna.*

"Have you had breakfast?" Carol asks. "I've got homemade cinnamon rolls!"

It's a friendly town, I surmise, and the people have a good sense of humor too — they lovingly call themselves the Lunatics. Of course, it's an apt name for those living in a place named Luna. But it's also a name invoking a creative imagination, tied to its translation — moon — the orb most associated with dreamers.

The day takes on a dreamy quality as all around me members of the Laney family savor luscious rolls with a scent of buttery cinnamon. I follow suit while Carol tells me a little history.

Her husband Joe's family — Mormon folk — helped settle the town back in the late 1800s. These first-comers to this mountainous area set up cattle ranches and small farms. Every year, they celebrate Pioneer Day in late July, when the first Mormons arrived in Salt Lake City following the dream of Brigham Young. That's why we're here today.

"All our life we raised our kids here," says Carol. "And they feel it's a special day to come home."

Indeed, with some 40 family members milling about, sleeping nights in tents and in the attic, it's a strong tradition. Other families share in the town's homecoming, parking their cars and pickup trucks on the main drag. They sit on tailgates and foldout canvas chairs, visiting and waiting for the parade to begin.

I head across the street to check out the local gallery, Annie's on the Corner (open in summer). It's set in a 150-year-old wooden home and features local landscape paintings,

*The Wild Cow Riding competition brings laughs as cowboys attempt to get stubborn cows down the length of the arena.*

antiques such as a pine and pressed-tin kitchen hutch and little copper saddle ornaments. The gallery also sells Double Blessings Goat Milk Soap, a bar of which I purchase just in time to hear horse hooves clomping on the pavement outside.

Under a bold sun, the parade marches on with rodeo marshals atop tall quarter horses and period automobiles sporting shiny fenders. A rusty green Sidewinder tractor chugs along, followed by a covey of kids on bikes and ribbon-draped cars filled with local politicians. Bringing up the rear, a big barbecue grill on wheels leaves a trail of smoke with the scent of mesquite.

After the last of the parade, I follow the grill to the community center, where I feast on barbecue beef, coleslaw and potato salad, finishing with apple cobbler. The dining hall is all business, with locals and visitors stoking up before heading off to the day's high point — the rodeo.

The rodeo setting is like none I've ever seen. Rather than a bare spot on a dusty prairie, it's tucked into the hills, surrounded by ponderosas. Dogs and kids skitter amongst the trees while a stereo blasts and riders perform the grand entry. It's quite a rodeo, with participants coming from all over the region and hundreds of spectators sitting in mottled shade. A roster of events ranges from bull riding to an egg toss.

The first event — the one Luna is renowned for — gets everyone laughing. It's the Wild Cow Riding competition. While the competitors try to get on their cows, one cowboy falls and gets dragged the length of the arena on his belly. In an attempt to help, his buddy jumps on top of him, which slows the cow not one bit. Finally, one rider crosses the finish line.

As the crowd cools from their laughter, I make my way around. I meet up with Krista Steed, from nearby Eagar, Ariz., as she prepares her horse to run barrels.

"My grandpa was raised up on a ranch," she says. "And I got into riding because of him." She wears a buckle with a barrel racer slanting on it and rides a finely tooled saddle, both of which she won in previous competitions.

"It's fun," she says. "Keeps your adrenaline rushing." She climbs on and runs her race, the crowd cheering as she clocks one of the fastest times on the chart.

The team roping, bull riding and egg toss continue on without mishap, except for a few broken yolks. Then comes the bronc-riding competition. A horse falls down out of the bucking chute and a cowboy lands underneath the animal and gets caught. A bullfighter jumps in, grabs the rein and hauls on it, so the horse gets up and the cowboy scrambles away. In a final fit of fury, the horse kicks, barely missing the cowboy's head.

The crowd cheers him out of the arena, and I do too, fully convinced of the fun and drama of this show. This village has succeeded in its vision: The event might be put on by Lunatics, but it definitely is the World's Biggest Small Town Rodeo.

Pioneer Day takes place in late July.

*Krista Steed, from nearby Eagar, Ariz., prepares to run her horse, Easy, in the barrels competition.*

## TORTUGAS: Lighting the Way for La Virgen

NIGHT, AND THE COLD OF WINTER SURROUND ME. SHADOWS OF OCOTILLO AND YUCCA STAND LIKE CHIHUAHUAN DESERT PHANTOMS AGAINST THE LIGHTS OF LAS CRUCES. I WAIT ALONE IN THE DARK.

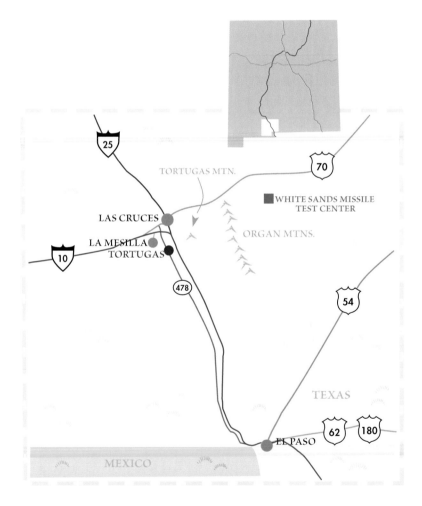

*Carrying* quiotes, *pilgrims (L to R) Cyndia Sandoval, Rebecca Mondragon, Fabian Mondragon, and Melinda Reyes make their way down from Tortugas Mountain.*

A fire burns on a hilltop, and silhouetted against its crimson shine, a man appears, then another. Some 60 people make their way down a dark road, many holding *quiotes* — staffs topped with the rosettes of yucca leaves, symbols of the roses that Juan Diego presented to La Virgen de Guadalupe. This is the Fiesta of Our Lady of Guadalupe in Tortugas.

Few people know of the little village of Tortugas. But it's a lively community that's fast being swallowed up by Las Cruces. Though the village itself is small, with a church on a dusty plaza and modest homes, its history is large and this ceremony brilliant.

Tortugas was settled in the mid-1800s by a mixture of people from Isleta Pueblo to the north and Isleta del Sur in Texas. Piro Indians and Mansos also joined in, as did Spanish-Americans and Mexican Indians, creating a variety of cultures whose main thread is Tiwa. Though not legally recognized as a pueblo, and with no land grants nor reservation, Tortugas has a very strong identity, upheld by a nonprofit organization called the *Corporacíon de los Indígenes de Nuestra Señora de Guadalupe*, more commonly referred to as The Corporation.

Each December the village celebrates the Feast Day of Guadalupe for three days, including a pilgrimage, a procession and dances. In its early years, more than a century ago, the pilgrimage crossed Chihuahuan Desert en route to Tortugas Mountain, also known to Las Cruces locals as "A" Mountain.

Today the journey is more technical and treacherous. Pilgrims travel east through their village, into a flood opening that passes under Interstate 10, across the New Mexico State University campus, and below Interstate 25. Then the journey breaks out into the desert and climbs Tortugas, a bald, turtle-shaped hill that's backed by the jagged peaks of the Organ Mountains in the distance.

The marchers travel up at dawn and spend the day atop the mountain, praying and making *quiotes*. Now, at dusk, they're at the base, where they ignite a bonfire to light the path of the Virgin, helping her come down the mountain for her annual visit. With staffs in hand, they stand before the building flames. They don't tarry, though. With almost five miles to walk back to the village, they begin to tread quietly, the only sounds a low rumble of conversation, the ring of a cell phone and a spark of laughter.

A local tells me that the pilgrims come from all over, returning home from Los Angeles or Denver to walk with their families. Rebecca Mondragon has made the trek every year for the past 10.

"We walked up with the Indians at 7:30 this morning," she says. "It's a sacrifice, like a promise to Our Lady."

Scholar Jacqueline Dunnington writes in *Viva Guadalupe!* that, indeed, pilgrimages such as this are not pious processions. "They are quests that involve a promise or vow," she writes. "Inspiration, comfort, and reinforcement of purpose come from the belief that Guadalupe is a pilgrim walking with them, a member of the extended community, a beloved relative at their side."

While the pilgrims walk with "*la Morena*," the Virgin, festivities have already started back in Tortugas Pueblo. Wearing costumes with bright ribbons, dancers ply the dusty plaza in front of the Shrine and Parish of Our Lady of Guadalupe. Meanwhile, the *mayordomos* of the village are busy making *albondigas* — meatballs — for the feast.

"We make 350 pounds of *albondigas*," says Felipe Chavez, who has helped with them for years, and invites me to join in rolling them.

The next day I see the dances in stark winter light. Long shadows play on the dust, the distant Organ Mountains topped with snow. The dancers are lively today, many dressed with the ominous bishop hoods of the *Matachines*. Surprisingly few visitors surround them. Here, there's little demarcation between the participants and the viewers, so I can get close and see into those deep brown eyes not quite hidden behind their masks.

The *Matachines* dances continue in front and in back of the church, fiddles scratching out the melody, while a drum pounds the rhythm. A little girl playing the part of *La Malinche* makes her way among the tall-hooded figures, as they dance out the story of good triumphing over evil. Snowflakes fall and visitors press against each other to stay warm. A shotgun blasts, keeping everyone jittery.

At midday the dances stop for a feast. The bishops remove their headdresses and lay them out on the hood of a car. Meanwhile, everyone lines up outside a community center waiting their turn to eat meatballs.

My fingers cold, but my head full of colorful images, I make my way out of Tortugas, through the modern city that surrounds the village, with Our Lady of Guadalupe's presence still with me.

*Dancers rhythmically wave blunt-tipped arrows to symbolize peace.*

*In front of Our Lady of Guadalupe Parish, dancers perform the Matachines Dance, which tells the story of good triumphing over evil.*

# Northwest

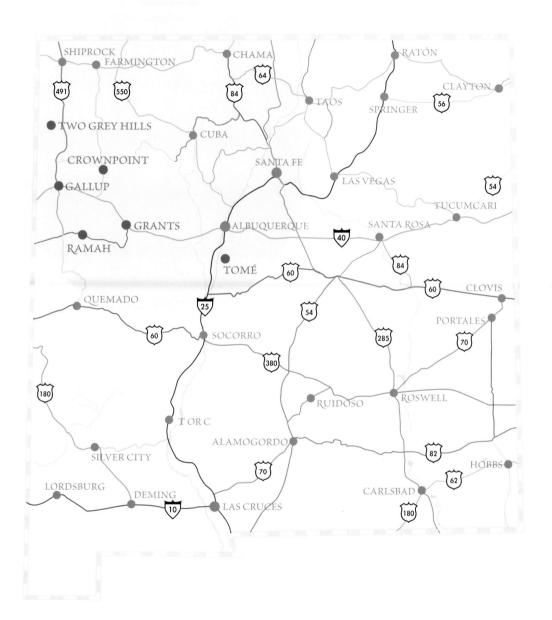

# CROWPOINT: A Navajo Carpet Ride

IN CROWNPOINT, THE LITTLE NAVAJO EN-CLAVE NEAR GALLUP, SWELTERING AIR FILLS AN ELEMENTARY SCHOOL GYMNASIUM, BUT NO ONE SEEMS TO NOTICE. THEY'RE TOO BUSY POLITELY ELBOWING THEIR WAY THROUGH THE CROWD, LOOKING AT RUGS.

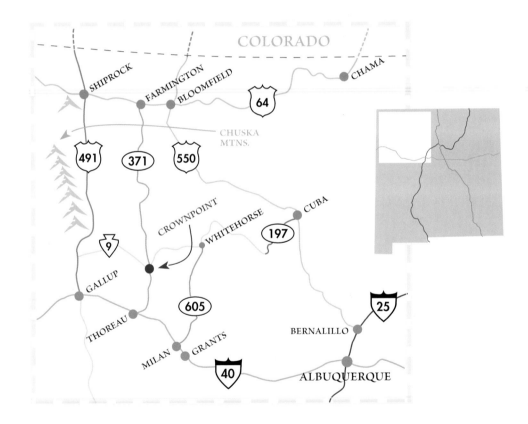

They measure and pinch them, hold them at arm's length and up to other rugs, all under the steady gaze of the weavers who made them.

This is only the beginning of a raucous night at the Crownpoint Rug Auction, a monthly event of mythic renown that draws together weavings from all over the Southwest and buyers from around the world. One warm Friday night, my mother and I hop on this Navajo carpet ride and cruise through a land of beauty and adrenaline.

A couple from France holds a rug this way and that, looking at each other and back at it. A woman from Las Vegas, Nev., — her fourth time at the auction this year — makes notes on a little pad. Meanwhile, a man from Albuquerque, who's been coming for 30 of the auction's 39 years, uses the foot-long floor tiles to check the size. Such are the buyers, the register listing a range of places: Dallas, Texas, La Jolla, Skull Valley, Ariz., and Rolla, Mont.

*A couple from France, Serge Devaux and Monique Hasle, examine a rug.*

A young Navajo woman watches intently with her husband, son and baby. Harriann Mariano traveled from nearby Standing Rock to sell a rug at the auction for the first time. She started weaving at age 10 under the instruction of her grandmother.

"She's been checking up on me all week making sure I'm doing a good job," says Harriann. "I'm kind of anxious because there's a lot of competition, especially from the older women."

With a crack on the microphone, one of the auction organizers, Christine Ellsworth, lays down the rules. She shows where to pay and where to pick up your purchase. "We can't take foreign checks," she says, "because it's hard to get them through the bank, but we'll still take checks from Texas." Laughter nudges through the crowd.

The bidding starts at $500 for a medium-sized rug with brilliant reds and blues. The

*A young weaver, Harriann Mariano, anticipates the beginning of the auction, with her baby, Shanti, son Marisano, and husband, Shawn.*

price quickly climbs to $1,950. Sold! A few more sell fast. Then the crowd hushes when a big Chinle rug of red and navy comes up. It sells easily for $1,700.

The auctioneer keeps rolling out the rugs and the numbers, and the sounds converge in my head in a mass of Navajo place names that sing like a ballad: Burnt Corn, Two Grey Hills, Kayenta, Indian Wells, Blue Gap and Many Farms.

People fan themselves with their auction numbers. They sit and stand, lining the walls, old and young, prim yuppies and road-dusty traders, filling every inch of space, while the weavers sit at picnic tables in the back, barely moving.

The auctioneer plays the crowd.

"Talk to me, sir, not to her," he jests, to a bidder who keeps conferring with his wife. "Five-fifty, now 600. Talk to me some more. Stand on your own two feet." The man and his wife buy the rug for $600.

Weavers put a minimum price on their rugs so that the works they've often spent months making don't undersell. A big red-and-black piece starts at $2,100. With no bidders, it will go to another sale or a dealer. Still, the rugs are dirt-cheap here, selling for one-third of what they would at a shop in Santa Fe.

"It's just money," says the auctioneer, encouraging a sale. There's a gambling tone here that gets in your blood and makes you want to stick a bidding card in the air, which is exactly why I don't have one. A woman from Houston says to me, "We get into a fever of bidding. In fact, my husband bidded against himself."

Auctioneers Wayne Connell and Delbert Artry work to drum up bids on a rug.

"Sold! For ten-hunnerd," barks the auctioneer, selling a rug for $1,000. Then he starts again on a medium-sized one with an eagle dancer in the middle. "Three seventy-five, four hunnerd, seventy-five, three seventy-five, four, four hunnerd, unnerd, unnerd, sold for four hunnerd."

As the rugs pass by, even a novice like me begins to see patterns — the light greens and browns of Many Farms, the inventive geometrics of Blue Gap. Some of them take your breath they are so lovely. A tiny one comes up and the auctioneer jokes kindly. "They went all out on that one." But the crowd sighs, in love with the piece, no larger than a glass coaster. It sells for $35.

Suddenly out of the maelstrom emerges a huge rug from Flagstaff, Ariz. Intricate and layered with imagery, it's a ballet of gray, red and black. The bidding starts hot, drumming up fast and my mom and I look at each other as it tops $2,000. It becomes a duel — two men working it — with the auctioneer driving the price higher. Finally, it sells for $2,350.

Granted it's not a lot of money, but that's just the point: The buyers get a complete treasure, as well as the thrill of wresting a rug from another's grasp.

On our way out, I see the young weaver Harriann, from Standing Rock. Her rug was pure poetry, a twining of blues and grays around a graceful figure. Unfortunately, the crowd didn't meet her $450 minimum. But she left with her eyes steady and proud. She still has her rug, and a lifetime of auctions before her.

# GALLUP FLEA MARKET:
## A Carnival of Delights

ON AN OPEN FIELD NORTH OF GALLUP, VEN-
DORS SET UP SHOP EVERY SATURDAY IN
WHAT HAS BECOME ONE OF NEW MEXICO'S
MOST RENOWNED AND EXOTIC OPEN-AIR
MARKETS.

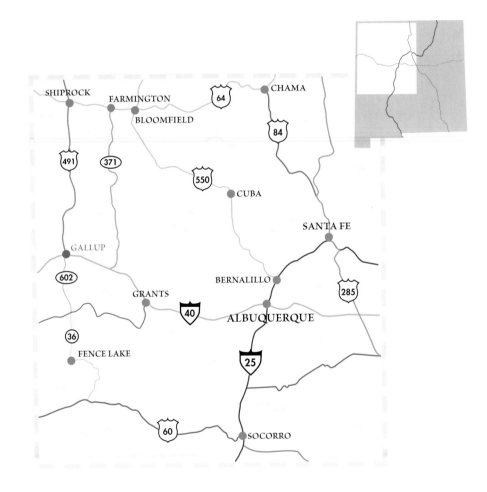

A t the Gallup Flea Market, an array of merchants sells everything from *katsina* dolls to sparkly snow globes, traditional blue corn cakes to Rice Krispies treats. It's a carnival of delights — natural, supernatural and plastic.

*A vendor who only likes to be called "Johnny" prepares* katsina *dolls.*

I arrive early, just as vendors set up shop. Already the sweet scent of glazed donuts flirts with the musky odor of mutton stew. At a booth, Fara Yazi greets me, her head wrapped in a tapestry and dark eyes shining in the morning sun.

"I've been doing this every Saturday for 20 years," she says, polishing a bracelet and setting it in a glass case. Then she fills me in on why she and many of the other vendors work here, a marketplace for over 20 years.

"You don't pay much rent. You don't have to open every day, and you make enough to support yourself for the whole week," she says. Sounds good to me.

A hawker calls me over, a tall, thin man who offers a free sample of a potion that's made with desert herbs. Before I can think, he's rubbing some on my arthritic wrist. "You leave that for awhile and come back and tell me how it feels," he says. I agree and head on, a little wary.

I enter the Navajo medicine lane, where a handful of women sell herbs. Stepping up to a table, I meet the gaze of a woman whose flat face is a highway map of her life. Before her on the table is a bag of "Lightening Medicine," with a tag instructing to boil one teaspoon in water and drink the mixture four times a day. Another bag contains *"His Yi Ya Nii,"* for internal infections, and another, "Traditional Tobacco," for good fortune and financial success.

I reach for a bag marked "Deer Way Smoke," and the woman swats my hand away. She and the others shoo me away like a gnat from the table — not enough Navajo running in my veins, I surmise.

The Touchines are friendlier. From nearby Church Rock, this Navajo family makes lovely jewelry often set with large turquoise stones. Like much of the jewelry at the market, it's bargain priced, but still made with great effort.

"When we're not here, we're pounding silver," says Angelina Touchine, smiling and

In the image, the following signs are visible:

Hot Cocoa .75

Bottled Water 20oz $1 25

CORN STEW $5 25
VEGETABLE STEW $5 25
DUMPLING STEW $5 25
Roast Mutton Sandwich $5 25
NAVAJO BURGER $5 25
HAMBURGER + chips $3 50
CHEESEBURGER + chips $3 75
FRYBRE a $1 25
T lla
NAVAJ A 50¢

BLUE MUSH $1 50

COKE 7UP
Diet Coke
SPRITE
PEPSI
Diet Pepsi
DR. PEPPER 75¢

COFFEE
.40  .60  1 00

*Jacina Benally graces the Benally family food concession.*

hugging her daughter, who helps her set bracelets and necklaces in the cases.

By now my wrist is tingly and warm. I'm still wary of the potion but no longer afraid that my skin will dissolve. I follow a familiar smell of bread frying into a food shack full of people eating at tables.

Sixteen-year-old Jacina Benally greets me. She leads me into the back to meet her grandmother, Alice Benally, who started selling food at the booth some 20 years ago. Today, the elder woman is cooking what she calls "fire bread" over a scalding pot of oil.

A dignified woman dressed in royal blue, Alice stretches the dough between her hands and then swings it out so it lands flat on the oil. She invites me back for lunch later and I promise to return.

Music lures me away, as Native American drumbeats and flutes play a contemporary rock melody. It comes from a tape booth with hundreds of titles including the one playing, called "Apache Jam," by Delmar Boni. In the distance, the potion hawker lifts his brows at me and rubs his own wrist — just checking up.

I stop in front of a couple chowing down on something foreign to me.

"Roast mutton sandwiches," they say, holding them out proudly. The woman gives me a rundown on her favorite flea market treat — a piece of Indian fry bread filled with mutton and topped with a long, unpeeled green chile. I admit it does smell good.

I swim through people of all sizes and types, past a truck full of colorful corn, then tables covered with plastic things — toy clowns and cars, umbrella hats and key chains, finding myself at herbalist Barbara Anne Johnson's makeshift tent. She sells her own con-

96

coctions whose names metaphorically illustrate their purposes — such as "Toro Tea," with ginseng, palmetto and horsetail, for men.

Out of the blue she asks if I'll watch her booth. "Sure," I say, trying to sound less uncertain than I am.

I sit down as though I own the place, watching people walk by, feeling the slight sense of rejection when they turn up their noses at "my" product, a sense of fulfillment when they're interested. They flow in a clockwise direction, with only a few stragglers going the opposite way — people like me who haven't quite learned the system.

Lamentably, I fail to sell anything for Barbara by the time she returns, but I do buy some sandalwood soap from her.

My lunch awaits me at the Benallys' booth. Just what I'd hoped for: a roast mutton sandwich. After thanking them, I bite into it, tasting the gamy flavor of the meat, mixed with the sweet bite of chile.

En route to my car, I catch the eye of the potion hawker. I touch my wrist. Yes, I nod at him, the pain is gone.

*Angelina and Brittany Touchine make and sell Navajo jewelry.*

## GRANTS:
Reincarnation of a Boom-Bust Town

WITHIN A SINGLE LIFETIME, MOST PEOPLE LIVE MANY INCARNATIONS. CAREER CHANGES, FAMILY SHIFTS AND TRAVEL ALL ADD TO THE JOURNEY'S RICHNESS. I FIND THAT PLACES ARE NO DIFFERENT.

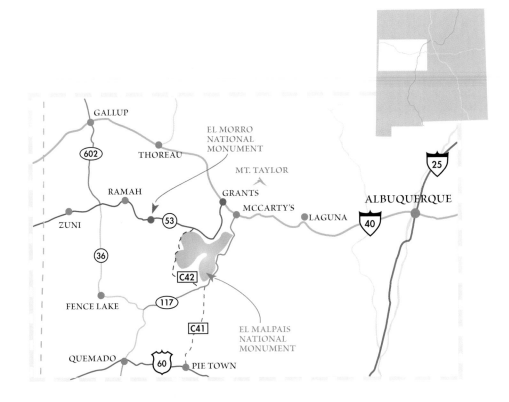

*Owners of The Mission at Riverwalk coffeehouse and gallery, Michael and Peggy Lewis, view Grants as a happening outdoors place.*

O n a trip to Grants in western New Mexico I get a glimpse of a town's bright new life. It's a cold winter day at the base of Mount Taylor. Winds blow swirling snow clouds off its 11,301-foot peak and, in its shadow, black lava flows stretch for thousands of acres to the south. Such is the dramatic setting for this story. At the New Mexico Mining Museum and Grants/Cíbola County Chamber of Commerce in the center of town, I meet up with Star Gonzales, a local with a bright smile and an attitude that seems to embody the new Grants.

Once the Cíbola County Queen, she's now executive director of the chamber. "I have a real passion for this community," she says. She also has a passion for golf, which she plays at the Coyote del Malpais, a course she calls "world class." And she also raises Colonial Spanish mustangs with her husband on the Elkin's Ranch, a pioneer-family spread on Mount Taylor. The attitude she carries that's so indicative of the new Grants is a penchant for fun.

"Newcomers see this as a small town at the base of a big mountain surrounded by national forest," says Michael Lewis, who along with his wife Peggy opened up The Mission at Riverwalk, a coffee house and gallery that serves delectables such as cappuccinos, lattes and chocolate-chunk cookies. "This fresh viewpoint is going to help our town go forward," he adds.

Indeed, Grants is a place surrounded by natural and historic wonders: El Malpais National Monument has some of the newest lava flows on the North American continent; Mount Taylor is home to one of the world's most demanding winter competitive events, the Mount Taylor Winter Quadrathlon; and El Morro National Monument displays, on a 200-foot-tall bluff, centuries of written record from those who passed through and inhabited this area. These are the new focus points for both incoming residents and travelers.

The new attitude is remarkable because of the town's previous incarnations. Grants is like a case study of a boom-and-bust town. Residents have weathered an early railroad ex-

*Inside the New Mexico Mining Museum's underground section, mining cars rest on tracks.*

istence and then "Carrot-Capital-of-the-Country" fame. Neon lit the town during its Route 66 heyday, with signs for the Uranium Café and Lavaland Motel still serving as reminders of the era. And it reached its financial zenith during the uranium mining days of the Cold War, when it was called "Uranium Capital of the World."

Bob Peets, who I meet up with at the museum, came to Grants at the height of the uranium boom to operate a mine for Phelps Dodge. "There was a shortage of housing back then," Bob says. "People were living in trailers and sheds, anywhere they could find."

In the museum, a photograph attests to the number of mining companies working the area. Direction arrows stand by a roadside pointing every which way: Atomic Uranium Inc., Continental Uranium Co., Lisbon Uranium Corp., Big Indian Mines and many more.

Other such pieces of history are on display at the museum, but the highlight here is the mock uranium mine underground. An elevator takes me down into a spooky, low-lit place with rough stone walls. I begin in the station where uranium is loaded and unloaded on tracks, and then I travel farther into the earth through places defined on wall plaques and explained by recordings of actual miners, their gritty voices blending with the scent of dust. The loss of that industry in the mid-1980s was a defeat for Grants that left a major malaise.

"For years everyone was still looking back at the bust," says Lawrence Sanchez, a local businessman and longtime resident, who I also meet at the museum. "But now people are really looking forward."

And there's plenty to look to. As well as The Mission at Riverwalk gallery, the town has the Double Six Gallery, which specializes in Spanish, cowboy and fine art. During my visit, a Mount Taylor retrospective hangs. The variety of views of the notable peak range from Roxanna Cronk's moody black-and-white painting with a single star in the sky to Michael Lewis' poetically lit verdant scene.

My next stop is the Northwest New Mexico Visitor Center east of town. In an expansive Pueblo-style building with a broad atrium showing off views of El Malpais, this place offers fliers and films on the region's parks, forests and Indian country. A real treat here is a series of suggested driving tours displayed with large color photos and free cards describing the routes.

One tour takes visitors along the volcanoes of El Malpais, another through the abandoned logging communities of the Zuni Mountains Historical Loop, and yet another to the stunning geologic formations of the Cabezón Peak and Río Puerco areas.

I finish my tour of Grants at the Sandstone Bluffs Overlook in El Malpais, one of my favorite views in the state. As I look out at the stark contrast between the sun-burnished cliffs sculpted by wind and rain and the tangled mass of black lava hundreds of feet below, I think about the new Grants. This incarnation, I surmise, will likely endure, since it relies on the area's most innate characteristic — its beauty.

*Sandstone Bluffs Overlook at El Malpais National Monument offers vast views of the badlands and Mount Taylor.*

## RAMAH: Weaving a Unique Vision

ON A SUMMERTIME SATURDAY IN WESTERN NEW MEXICO, LOCALS SIT UNDER SHADE TREES SIPPING DARK COFFEE WHILE EATING HAZELNUT COOKIES AND RASPBERRY TARTS. LIVE GUITAR MUSIC LILTS OUT ACROSS IRRIGATED FIELDS WHERE HORSES AND CATTLE GRAZE.

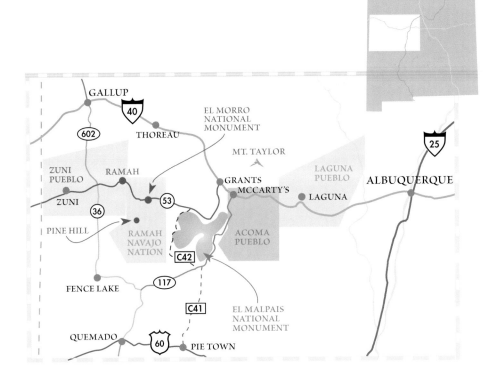

T his is what a visitor might find in Ramah, a place where people fearlessly create their own unique world. My father and I pass through the area one sunny day and take the time to stop.

*Settled in 1883, Ramah has many historical buildings.*

The pastoral café scene is part of the Ramah Farmers Market, where locals bring their creations to sell. Lettuce, spinach, beets, onions and carrots sit on tables and in bins amid the honey-like scent of flowers — snapdragons, cosmos and sweet pea blossoms. Zuni fetishes, hand-made dolls and weavings also adorn tabletops.

Kate Wilson, who manages the market, helped create this idyllic scene. Fifteen years ago, she and her husband, Andy, moved here from southeast Texas. Throughout the years, with their help and that of many others, the region developed the El Morro Area Arts Council, which now sponsors events every week that range from this market to music performances to art shows to open-mike nights.

"It's been nice to be part of bringing in the things you want in your community," says Kate.

This area has always had a strong consciousness about what it wants in life. It's bordered by the reservation lands of Zuni Pueblo and the Ramah band of the Navajo Nation. Both tribes are known for their fierce independence.

The town of Ramah, which was settled by Mormons in 1883, still is a predominantly Mormon town even though the region's residents come from a broad mix of ancestors, including Texas bean farmers and Spanish sheepherders.

Much of this story is told at the Ramah Historical Museum. Set in a 1902 stone building at the center of town, the museum offers exhibits of the area's Native American and Mormon history. It's the vision of Paul Merrill, who grew up here, left for 60 years then returned home with a dedication to help the community.

"Ramah didn't have a library, park or museum," Paul says. I've been working on those ever since." But he doesn't like to take the credit. "A person has lots and lots of help," he adds, and he thanks the community members and his late wife, Patti Merrill.

*Artists Pamela Davis and Lisa de St. Croix exhibit paintings at the Old School Gallery outside Ramah.*

From the museum, we head east of town on scenic N.M. 53 to the Old School Gallery. With buffed hardwood floors and clean white walls, it's a surprising find out amongst the sandstone monoliths and piñon trees. Here, in this old schoolhouse, area artists display their work.

One such person, Pamela Davis, an energetic woman with bright brown eyes, is a native of the area. Pamela's grandfather, a Mormon homesteader, came here in 1914 and she was raised as a Mormon. But as Pamela grew older, she left the church.

"It's a good thing that unifies people," she says of the religion. Then she adds with a wry smile, "When I went to college and started thinking, I was no longer a Mormon."

Some of her paintings depict the area, evoking a sense of its remoteness and yet a spiritual brightness. "It's great for me to experience the light and see if I can capture it," she says.

From the gallery, we travel south across the Ramah Navajo reservation-allotted lands. This band of Navajos is known for self-determination, demonstrated in their insistence on a separate existence from the rest of the Navajo Nation in eastern Arizona and western New Mexico, and for creating one of the first Indian-controlled schools in the United States. We drive along open prairie and then climb into ponderosa forest to Pine Hill in search of the newest addition to the area's creative scene — a gallery.

Yin-May Lee, an athletic, matter-of-fact woman, greets us outside some portable school buildings where she works for Ramah Navajo Continuing Education. She describes the

*Near Ramah, sandstone mesas paint the landscape.*

origin of a new hogan that the Ramah Navajo Weavers Association and friends are building — a place where weavers can convene to work and learn together.

"We wanted to have a home for the weaving," Yin-May says. "The word 'hogan,' in Navajo, 'hooghan,' means home — a place to rejuvenate the beauty, to restore harmony."

The project is experimental. To build the structure, volunteers participated in a pilot program sponsored by the U.S. Forest Service, cutting small-diameter wood from overgrown forests in the region. "We wondered how the community could tap into a resource that's readily available," says Yin-May.

As well as teaching in the hogan, weavers will display rugs there. These rare works are woven from the wool of Navajo-owned churro sheep, which is especially soft, with long fibers. Once the wool is prepared, the weavers use natural dyes obtained from such things as indigo, cactus beetles and rabbit brush to create dynamic designs — triangles, crosses and thunderclouds in deep browns, tans and blacks, accented with turquoise, magenta and yellow.

Saying goodbye to Yin-May, we make our way toward home. We pass El Morro National Monument, where for centuries Native Americans, the Spanish, American Territorial-era soldiers and other travelers inscribed messages on rock. The sight of the etched sandstone face rising up into a blue evening sky seems apropos in a place where so many continue to make their creative mark.

# A HILL
ISN'T JUST
A HILL
IN TOMÉ

IN NEW MEXICO, NOTHING IS SIMPLE. A RIVER ISN'T JUST A RIVER, IT'S THE RÍO GRANDE — THE BIG OR GREAT RIVER, FLOWING WITH A THOUSAND CONNOTATIONS. SIMILARLY, A HILL ISN'T JUST A HILL, OR SO WE FIND ONE DAY ON A JOURNEY TO TOMÉ.

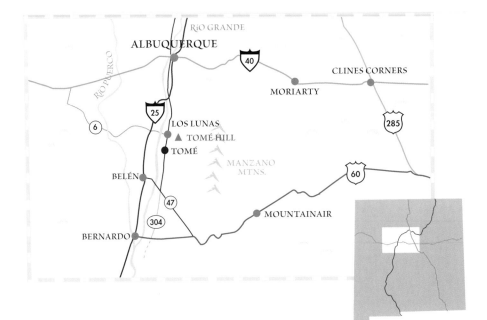

*Immersed in prayer, Juan Maestas, from Jarales, carries a makeshift cross toward the hilltop.*

**W**hen I first heard about Tomé Hill, I thought, "So?" It's a hill, south of Los Lunas, rising 1,200 feet above the Río Grande Valley. I mean, we have mountains in New Mexico. Of what interest could be a little hill?

Despite my cynicism, my father and I set out one day at the end of a wet storm with the intent of climbing this hill. Little did I know when I invited him along that he and his wife had spent quite a bit of time in Tomé with Edwin Berry, who's part of the Baca family that's lived in the area for generations.

We've chosen to travel on Good Friday, so the shoulders of N.M. 47 are dotted with pilgrims walking toward the hill. Suddenly we see it between the cottonwoods, a gently rounded hump with three crosses on top. My father explains that Edwin Berry and other area *penitentes* erected the crosses in 1948. Though Edwin is deceased, we have plans to visit his widow today.

But first we head to the Church of Our Lady of the Immaculate Conception on the Tomé Plaza. Though built in 1750, the church has been renovated many times since, so the outside appears modern. But the inside retains an ancient cathedral feel, with *vigas* on the ceiling and high, bright stained-glass windows letting in magical light. Next door, a little museum displays chalices, silver incense thuribles and a blessing signed in 1865 by Roman Catholic Archbishop Jean Baptiste Lamy.

The Plaza is a broad grassy court studded with the church on one side and a vacant 1875 adobe jail on the other. It's easy to imagine village life centering here. Pueblo tribes first inhabited the region, then the Spanish conquest brought settlers. One of the first was Tomé Domínguez de Mendoza, for whom the hill and town were named. Others followed him, digging a vast network of *acequias* and tilling the land to plant wheat, beans and corn. Today, the village is still agrarian based, with farmers growing alfalfa and tending cattle.

Next, we make our way to the Berry home, where Edwin's widow, Assunta, welcomes us into her kitchen. She's a noble Italian woman with large features, short salt-and-pepper hair, and hands loud with gestures. We sit at her bright table surrounded by the rich scent of baking bread.

*The top of Tomé Hill offers views across central New Mexico.*

She tells us in a lively mixture of Italian, Spanish and English that during World War II she and Edwin met in "Napoli" or Naples, Italy. "My papa was working with the Americans," Assunta says, while serving us what she calls *casatello*, the bread we smelled. She bakes it for Easter, with whole eggs embedded in the top. I note a rich taste and ask her to reveal the special ingredient.

"Pure lard," she replies.

"Of course!" I say.

Bidding her goodbye, we head to the hill. We're not alone as we make our way up the rocky path. More than a thousand pilgrims accompany us, some walking barefoot, some carrying crosses, a few talking on cell phones. It's a brilliantly colored procession that snakes before us, voices saying, "*cuidado, cuidado*" (careful, careful) to children. One woman stops with her tiny grandson and says slowly, "With the father, the son and the holy spirit." Turning to us, she explains, "He's learning the 'Our Father,' today."

With tired lungs, we reach the summit, where all kinds of people — children and very old grandmothers, teenagers and biker types, look off in the distance at the Manzano Mountains or at the lovely thread of green that is the Río Grande. They kneel by the shrine, raise arms in supplication and sing along with a little guitar band playing hymns.

I wander away from the crowd and find remnants of Native American history: stones set in the shape of rooms, a rock ring and farther down the hill still, petroglyphs depicting a lizard, a coyote and Kokopelli playing his flute. In all, some 1,800 petroglyphs decorate the black basalt at various places on the hill.

We take the south route down, a steeper way that leads to the Tomé Hill Park. Here, an iron sculpture by Armando Álvarez depicts the history of the area, with Native Americans, conquistadors, missionaries, settlers and traders all marching through an arch.

Heading southerly toward the car, we pass ruts of *El Camino Real* marking the scrub. We turn for a last look up at the hill. Now, with our legs fatigued, it looks like a mountain, and, with my mind and heart full of its story, I know it truly is a *cerro grande* — a big or great hill.

*On Good Friday, Tomé Hill is covered with religious pilgrims.*

*Petroglyphs adorn many rocks along the western side of Tomé Hill.*

# MYSTERY BECOMES CONTROVERSY AT TWO GREY HILLS

A FRIEND AND I HEAD OUT ONE DAY UNDER A CLEAR NEW MEXICO SKY TO FIND THE FABLED PLACE, TWO GREY HILLS. I'D HEARD THE NAME — SYNONYMOUS WITH FINE NAVAJO WEAVING — SINCE I WAS A CHILD AND WALKED ON THE GREYS AND BROWNS OF A RUG MY FATHER BOUGHT 50 YEARS AGO, BEST OF SHOW AT THE NAVAJO NATION FAIR.

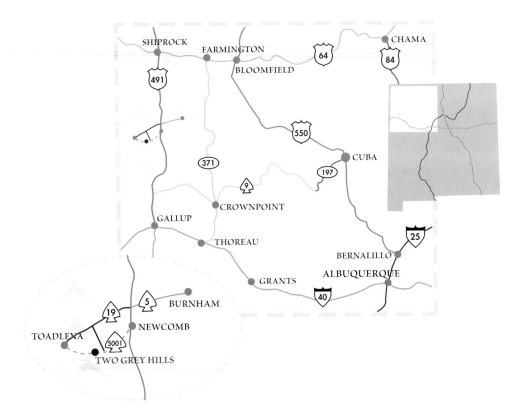

*En route to Two Grey Hills, many promontories pose as the location's possible namesake.*

*A*nd yet, all I knew of the rug's origin was some small place in western New Mexico.

Two Grey Hills — with a name that plain and literal, it ought to be easy to find. We drive north from Gallup.

"You think that's one of the hills?" my friend asks, pointing west.

"Maybe that's it," I say, indicating another rise.

When we turn off the highway, we still aren't sure, but after a short distance, we come upon a humble adobe building with a sign that reads "Two Grey Hills, est. 1897." Trader Les Wilson greets us and shows us past shelves full of corn flakes, gas cans, and bundles of yarn in rich greys and browns to a back room full of rugs. They aren't lit up with bright reds or startling blues, but they are beautiful, with a softness that comes from the wool's pure state.

"It's all naturally colored and handspun yarn," Wilson says. That's the secret of Two Grey Hills, one reason the rugs cost more than your average Navajo weaving. The many hues come not from dyes, but from the actual color of the sheep that grow the wool.

We ask about the mystery — which ones are the two grey hills?

"You can only see them if you're walking in the wash, which is the old wagon route here," he says. "We're on top of the two grey hills." He takes us out back where we overlook the arroyo he's referring to. Little do we know, that's not the end of the story.

What becomes apparent is that Two Grey Hills is really an area, with this post at its center. There's no town as one might suspect. The weavers, some 200 or so, live widely scattered. As was the case with most trading posts, this opened as a country store, offering goods or money for as-yet unfinished rugs, paying off when they were complete.

Smug with the fact that we solved the mystery, we head on to another trading post that serves the area in Toadlena, just a few miles west. Here, at the base of the Chuska Mountains, the Historic Toadlena Trading Post & Museum, dating back to 1909, stands as a showcase, a piece of history not to be missed. Within it, the other reason for Two Grey Hills rugs' fame comes clear — it's the artistry of the weavers.

*Trader Patty Morris oversees the register at the historic Toadlena Trading Post & Museum.*

The trader there, Patty Morris, leads us across worn wooden floors past shelves of bubble gum and canned mutton to the museum displaying what they call a Master Weavers' exhibit. Here, delicate heirloom rugs hang behind glass, a distinct mothball scent in the air. We see works by Rose Blueeyes, Edith Yazzie and many more, each with its own style, but with some patterns echoing like classic jazz riffs — double diamond, three column and storm.

Back at the front of the store, we find a woman dressed in deep purple, her brown face lined with age. She introduces herself as Clara Sherman, one of the master weavers of Two Grey Hills who is here this morning to buy groceries. "She comes every day," says the trader Patty.

Clara takes my arm and leads me back to a spot in the store where her rugs hang — large ones with bold, intricate patterns, each design resonating poetically throughout the piece. "These are all from my head," she says, claiming a workmanship that is often copied.

Weaving was something Clara had to fight for as a young girl, and it's apparent that she continues to fight today, at age 90. She struggles against arthritis in her fingers at a time

*Clara Sherman, a Two Grey Hills master weaver, stands in front of her creations.*

when her rugs are so accomplished that she won the 2004 Lifetime Achievement Award from the Southwest Association for Indian Arts.

She started weaving when she was 13, here, surrounded by the dust, sage and hills. "I had no wool," she says. "I'd chase sheep under the barbed wire fence and take it from there." She chuckles at the memory. I can see her, an agile young girl, collecting wool off barbed wire, and carding and spinning it by hand.

Clara looks up from our conversation, out the door, and our eyes follow hers. The sun is casting against two small mesas to the east, lovely hills that are a myriad of colors, from pink to maroon, with a hint of grey.

"Two Grey Hills," Patty says behind us. Clara motions to them, different ones from those mentioned earlier. These are prominent, like hills one would name a place after. Who do we believe? Maybe both renditions are true, and there are other even more notable hills in the area that could also be the two grey ones.

We may never know.

🍽 = dining      ⮧ = lodging

## North Central

### ARROYO SECO

Arroyo Seco is located on N.M. 150, 6 miles north of Taos.

🍽  Abe's Cantina y Cocina
489 N.M. 150, Arroyo Seco
(505) 776-8516

🍽  Gypsy 360° Café
480 N.M. 150, Seco Plaza, Arroyo Seco
(505) 776-3166

⮧  There are a number of great inns surrounding Arroyo Seco. For listings contact the Taos County Chamber of Commerce, (800) 732-8267 or (505) 758-3873. www.taoschamber.com

⮧  Little Tree Bed & Breakfast
226 Hondo Seco Road, Taos, N.M. 87513
(800) 334-8467, (505) 776-8467
www.littletreebandb.com

⮧  Abominable Snowmansion Skier's Hostel
476 N.M. 150, Arroyo Seco, N.M. 87571
(505) 776-8298
http://taoswebb.com/hotel/snowmansion

### CHAMA

For more information on activities in Chama, contact the Chama Valley Chamber of Commerce, 2372 N.M. 17, (800) 477-0149 or (505) 756-2306. www.chamavalley.com

🍽  Cookin' Books
2449 U.S. 84/64, at the "Y" in Chama
(505) 756-1717

🍽  High Country Restaurant & Saloon
Main Street (1/10 mile north of the "Y"), Chama
(505) 756-2384

⮧  Chama Station Inn
423 Terrace Ave., Chama N.M. 87520
(888) 726-8150, (505) 756-2315
info@chamastationinn.com

⮧  River Bend Lodge
2625 U.S. 64/84, Chama, N.M. 87520
(800) 288-1371
www.chamariverbendlodge.com

### COSTILLA & AMALIA

🍽  Gypsy 360° Café
480 N.M. 150, Seco Plaza, Arroyo Seco
(505) 776-3166

🍽  Orlando's New Mexican Café
114 Don Juan Valdez Lane, Taos
(505) 751-1450

⮧  There are a number of great inns 45 miles south of Costilla in the Taos area. For listings contact the Taos County Chamber of Commerce, (800) 732-8267, (505) 758-3873. www.taoschamber.com

⮧  Historic Río Plaza Inn and Retreat Center
N.M. 196, Costilla, N.M. 87524
(505) 586-9623

Little Tree Bed & Breakfast
County Road B-143 , Taos, N.M. 87513
(800) 334-8467, (505) 776-8467
www.littletreebandb.com

Check in at the Santa Fe National Forest Coyote
Ranger District to obtain maps and advice on access
to 60 miles of trails in the San Pedro Wilderness.
The office is located between Coyote and Gallina,
(505) 638-5526. For a guided hike, call Cerro Blanco
Adventures, (505) 638-5462.

Papa Joe's
N.M. 96 in Gallina
(505) 638-5525

Abiquiú Inn
21120 U.S. 84, Abiquiú, N.M. 87510
(505) 685-4378, www.abiquiuinn.com

Rancho de San Juan
34020 U.S. 285 (en route to Ojo Caliente)
Española, N.M. 87533
(505) 753-6818, www.ranchodesanjuan.com

*Poshuoninge* is located 1 mile west of the intersection
of U.S. 84 and N.M. 554. For information about area
art and the El Rito Studio Tour, visit
www.elritostudiotour.org.

El Farolito
1212 Main St., El Rito
(505) 581-9509

Abiquiú Inn
21120 U.S. 84, Abiquiú, N.M. 87510
(505) 685-4378, www.abiquiuinn.com

Rancho de San Juan
34020 U.S. 285 (en route to Ojo Caliente)
Española, N.M. 87533
(505) 753-6818, www.ranchodesanjuan.com

Pueblo Independence Day takes place in mid-
August from 10 a.m. to 5 p.m. For information
call (505) 829-3530. Food and refreshments are
available at the celebration.

Los Ojos Restaurant & Saloon
On N.M. 4 in Jémez Springs
(505) 829-3547

Laughing Lizard Inn & Café
17526 N.M. 4, Jémez Springs, N.M. 87025
(505) 829-3108, www.thelaughinglizard.com

Cañon del Río - Riverside Inn
16445 N.M. 4, Jémez Springs, N.M. 87025
(505) 829-4377, www.canondelrio.com

Clayton Lake State Park hosts star parties
throughout the year. For a schedule, call
(505) 374-8808. www.nmparks.com

The Eklund Hotel Dining Room & Saloon
15 Main St., Clayton, N.M. 88415
(877) 355-8631, www.theeklund.com

Best Western Kokopelli Lodge
702 S. First St., Clayton, N.M. 88415
(800) 528-1234, (505) 374-2589
www.bestwestern.com

| Rabbit Ear Café | Best Western Sands |
402 North First St. , Clayton, N.M.
(505) 374-3277

PUERTO DE LUNA

| Joseph's Restaurant & Cantina
865 Historic Route 66, Santa Rosa, N.M.
(505) 472-3361

La Quinta
1701 Historic Route 66, Santa Rosa, N.M. 88435
(800) 531-5900, (505) 472-4800
www.laquinta.com

**WHAT TO READ**

*Bless Me Ultima* by Rudolfo Anaya

RATÓN

The Ratón Museum is located at 216 S. First St.
and is open April through September, Tuesday
through Saturday, 9 a.m. to 5 p.m.; October
through March, Wednesday through Saturday,
10 a.m. to 4 p.m. Call (505) 445-8979.
The Ratón Arts and Humanities Council is
located at 145 S. First St.
Call (505) 445-2052.

| Oasis Restaurant
1445 S. Second St.
(505) 445-2221

| Pappas' Sweet Shop Restaurant
1201 S. Second St.
(505) 445-9811

Heart's Desire Antiques and Bed & Breakfast
301 S. Third St., Ratón, N.M. 87740
(866) 488-1028, (505) 445-1000

Best Western Sands
300 Clayton Highway, Ratón, N.M. 87740
(800) 518-2581, (800) 528-1234, (505) 445-2737

ROCIADA

Pendaries Village Mountain Resort
(open spring through fall)
1 Lodge Road, Rociada, N.M. 87742
(800) 733-5267, www.pendaries.net

Plaza Hotel
230 Plaza, Las Vegas, N.M. 87701
(800) 328-1882, (505) 425-3591
www.plazahotel-nm.com

El Rialto Restaurant and Lounge
141 Bridge St., Las Vegas, N.M.
(505) 454-0037

Star Hill Inn
County Road A-3, Sapello, N.M. 87745
(505) 425-5605, www.starhillinn.com

# Southeast

BLACKWATER DRAW

For information and directions, contact the Blackwater Draw Site at (505) 356-5235 or the museum
at (505) 562-2202. The site is located on N.M. 467,
5 miles north of U.S. 70. The museum is located on
U.S. 70, 5 miles north of Portales.

Cattle Baron
1600 S. Avenue D, Portales
(505) 356-5587

🍽 Something Different Grill
805 W. Second St., Portales
(505) 356-1205

🛏 Holiday Inn Express
1901 W. Second St., Portales, N.M. 88130
(800) 465-4329, (505) 356-4723

🛏 Super 8 Motel - Portales
1805 W. Second St., Portales, N.M. 88130
(800) 800-8000, (505) 356-8518
www.super8.com

Christmas on the Pecos runs nightly, Thanksgiving
through New Year's Eve, except for Christmas Eve.
For reservations and information, (505) 628-0952.
www.christmasonthepecos.com
The boats depart from the Pecos River Village.

🍽 Blue House
609 N. Canyon Rd., Carlsbad
(505) 628-0555

🍽 Lucy's
701 S. Canal St., Carlsbad
(505) 887-7714

🛏 Best Western Stevens Inn
1829 S. Canal St., Carlsbad, N.M. 88220
(800) 730-2851, (800) 528-1234, (505) 887-2851
www.bestwestern.com

🛏 Comfort Inn
2429 W. Pierce St., Portales, N.M. 88220
(800) 228-5150, (505) 887-1994
www.choicehotels.com

The annual Western Heritage Days takes place
in mid-June. For information call the Cloudcroft
Chamber of Commerce at (505) 682-2733.
www.cloudcroft.net

🍽 Dave's Café
300 Burro Ave., Cloudcroft
(505) 682-2127

🍽🛏 The Lodge at Cloudcroft
1 Corona Place, Cloudcroft, N.M. 88317
(800) 395-6343, (505) 682-2566
www.thelodgeresort.com

🛏 RavenWind Bed and Breakfast
1234 N.M. 24 (28 miles southeast of Cloudcroft)
Weed, N.M. 88354
(505) 687-3073, www.ravenwindranch.com

The Western Heritage Center & Lea County
Cowboy Hall of Fame is located at 5317 Lovington
Highway, (505) 492-2676. Information on Curtis
Fort's bronzes is available at www.curtisfort.com
or by calling (505) 398-6423.

🍽 Cattle Baron Steak and Seafood Restaurant
1930 N. Grimes St., Hobbs
(505) 393-2800

🍽 La Fiesta
604 E. Broadway, Hobbs
(505) 397-1235

🛏 Holiday Inn Express
3610 N. Lovington Highway
Hobbs, N.M. 88240

## GILA

🍽 Country Garden Café
8394 U.S. 180, Cliff
(505) 535-2545

↘ Casitas de Gila Guesthouses
50 Casita Flats Road, Gila, N.M. 88038
(877) 923-4827, www.casitasdegila.com

↘ Double E Guest Ranch
P.O. Box 280, Gila, N.M. 88038
(505) 535-2048, www.doubleeranch.com

↘ Gila River House
P.O. Box 131, Gila, N.M. 88038
(505) 535-2383, www.gilariverhouse.com

## LAKE ROBERTS

The Hummingbirds of New Mexico Festival takes place every few years. The weekend includes talks, guided walks, arts and crafts booths and baked goods for sale. For information call (505) 536-3866. www.hbnm.org

🍽↘ Grey Feathers Lodge
N.M. 35 and N. M. 15 in Lake Roberts
HC 68, Box 134, Silver City, N.M. 88061
(505) 536-3206, www.greyfeathers.com

🍽↘ Spirit Canyon Lodge & Café
684 N.M. 35 (mile marker 22), near Lake Roberts
HC 68, Box 60 , Silver City, N.M. 88061
(505) 536-9459, www.spiritcanyon.com

↘ Lake Roberts Cabins & General Store
869 N.M. 35, HC 68, Box 195,
Silver City, N.M. 88061
(505) 536-9929, www.lakeroberts.com

↘ Lake Roberts Motel
863 N.M. 35 (4 Miles south of the junction of
N.M. 15 and N.M. 35), Lake Roberts, N.M. 88061
(505) 536-9393

## LUNA

🍽 Río Frisco Barbecue
Main Street, Reserve, N.M.
(505) 533-6596

🍽 Ella's Café
Main Street, Reserve, N.M.
(505) 533-6111

↘ Rode Inn Motel
200 Main St., Reserve, N.M. 87830
(505) 533-6661

↘ Rivers Inn Bed & Breakfast (open in summer)
Off N.M. 435, P.O. Box 167
Reserve, N.M. 87830
(888) 235-2333

## TORTUGAS

🍽 Double Eagle
2355 Calle de Guadalupe
on the east side of Old Mesilla Plaza
(505) 523-6700

🍽 Chopes Bar & Café
N.M. 28 (in the center of town in La Mesa;
15 minutes south of Tortugas)
(505) 233-3420, (505) 233-9976

**Hotel Encanto de Las Cruces**
705 South Telshor Blvd., Las Cruces, N.M. 88011
(505) 522-4300, www.hotelencanto.com

**The Lundeen Inn of the Arts**
618 S. Alameda Blvd., Las Cruces, N.M. 88005.
(888) 526-3326, (505) 526-3326
www.innofthearts.com

**WHAT TO READ**
*Viva Guadalupe!*
By Jacqueline Orsini Dunnington

# Northwest

## CROWNPOINT

The Crownpoint Rug Weavers Association holds 12 auctions per year, normally on Friday evenings. For a schedule, call (505) 786-5302 or check the *New Mexico Magazine* "Sundial" calendar.

At the auction: Vendors sell tasty Navajo tacos, but buy yours early, as they tend to sell out.

**La Ventana**
110 1/2 Geis St., Hillcrest Center, Grants
(505) 287-9393

**Earl's**
1400 E. 66 Ave., Gallup
(505) 863-4201

**El Rancho Hotel and Motel**
1000 E. 66 Ave., Gallup, N.M. 87301
(800) 543-6351, (505) 863-9311
www.elranchohotel.com

**The Mission Guest House**
422 W. Santa Fe Ave., Grants, N.M. 87020
(505) 285-4632, www.grantsmission.com

## GALLUP

The Gallup Flea Market is located on North 9th Street (take U.S. 491 north of Gallup; turn east on Jefferson and continue to 9th Street). It's open on Saturdays from around 8 a.m. to sunset. For information call (800) 242-4282.

The Gallup Flea Market, of course!

**Jerry's Café**
406 W. Coal Ave., Gallup
(505) 722-6775

**El Rancho Hotel and Motel**
1000 E. 66 Ave., Gallup, N.M. 87301
(800) 543-6351, (505) 863-9311
www.elranchohotel.com

**La Quinta**
675 Scott Ave., Gallup, N.M. 87401
(800) 531-5900, (505) 327-4706
www.laquinta.com

## GRANTS

For information on Grants area attractions, contact the Grants/Cíbola County Chamber of Commerce at (800) 748-2142.
www.grants.org

**El Cafecito**
820 E. Santa Fe Ave., Grants
(505) 285-6229

🍽 La Ventana
110 Geis St., Hillcrest Center, Grants
(505) 287-9393

🛏 The Mission Guest House
422 W. Santa Fe Ave., Grants, N.M. 87020
(505) 285-4632, www.grantsmission.com

🛏 Cíbola Outpost Bed and Breakfast
1704 Enchanted Mesa, Grants, N.M. 87020
(866) 770-2486, (505) 287-4788
www.cibolaoutpost.com

## TOMÉ

Tomé is 5 miles south of Los Lunas on N.M. 47. To get to Tomé Hill, turn east on Tomé Hill Road and travel one-half mile. The Los Lunas Visitor Center has brochures with valuable information about the area. Call (505) 352-3596 or stop in at 3447 Lambros in Los Lunas.

🍽 Teofilo's Restaurante
144 Main St., Los Lunas
(505) 865-5511

🍽 Luna Mansion
110 Main St., Los Lunas
(505) 865-7333

🍽 Pete's Café
105 N. First St., Belén
(505) 864-4811

🛏 Roadrunner Roost Bed & Breakfast
72 Silva Rd., Tomé, N.M. 87060
(505) 865-7166, www.roadrunnerroost.com

🛏 Holiday Inn Express
2110 Camino del Llano, Belén, N.M. 87002
(888) 465-4329, (505) 861-5000
www.hiexpress.com

## TWO GREY HILLS

Two Grey Hills Trading Post (505-789-3270) and Toadlena Trading Post & Museum (505-789-3267) are located off U.S. 491 between Gallup and Shiprock, then about 7 miles on Indian Route 19.

🍽 Earl's
1400 E. 66 Ave., Gallup
(505) 863-4201

🍽 The Bluffs
3450 E. Main St., Farmington
(505) 325-8155

🛏 Casa Blanca
505 E. La Plata St., Farmington, N.M. 87401
(800) 550-6503, (505) 327-6503
www.casablancanm.com

🍽🛏 El Rancho Hotel and Motel
1000 E. 66 Ave., Gallup, N.M. 87301
(800) 543-6351, (505) 863-9311
www.elranchohotel.com